COYOTE

(Human Trafficker)

By Sheryl Recinos

Water Bear Press, Los Angeles, CA.
Water Bear Creed: Strong characters, hope, and resilience make the world a better place. Give more than you get. Change the world, one person at a time.

Paperback ISBN: 978-1-951542-17-7
E-book ISBN: 978-1-951542-18-4

This is a fictional depiction of current issues affecting youth in the United States and abroad. All characters are fictional, and any resemblance to real persons is coincidental.

For Byron, who never planned to come to the U.S, but came here anyway to save his life. Had you not made that journey, we never would have met. I am grateful that you survived, and forever thankful for our wonderful children.

PART ONE
US BORDER

ONE

"Shayla, I'm hungry," Brenden's voice startles me out of sleep. I'm usually a light sleeper, but I've been having strange nightmares all week. Papi says that he had a stretch of bad nightmares once too, right before my parents had to come to the United States.

I open my eyes and glance across the small bedroom that I share with both of my little brothers. He's on the top bunk, and Esteban is on the bottom. "Hey, Brenden," I say. He sits up and stretches his little arms before scurrying down the ladder of his bunk bed. Before I can even invite him to come cuddle next to me, he's squeezed himself under my covers and wrapped his arms around me in a bear hug.

"School starts next week," I remind him. He sighs, but then nods slowly. I ruffle his thick, black hair through my fingers.

"Do you maybe have an extra dollar?" he asks. He always asks me for an extra dollar or two; Brenden loves these really spicy chips called Takis. I secretly think he prefers them over Hot Cheetos because they're from Guatemala, like our parents. It's one of the few things that defines us as different, and my little brothers cling to it.

His big brown eyes are wide and full of mischief as he stares at me. "Please?" he adds.

"Alright," I say quietly. I make a few dollars each week when I help out at the diner with my mom, and I've been saving all summer for race fees. Some of my team's cross country meets require race fees to pay for the bus ride or the special t-shirts that they hand out at the meets. "After breakfast."

Brenden grins, and I can't help but smile back. "Thank you, thank you, thank you," he says cheerfully.

"Brenden," I hear Esteban call out from underneath a thick blanket. Our other brother pulls back the covers and stares at us both. "Can't you let me sleep in, just this once?" he groans.

I laugh, and Brenden jumps out of bed and throws his arms into the air. "I'm getting Takis!" he says.

"Shh!" I warn him. "Don't let Mami hear you," I scold as I stand up from my bed. If she knew that half of my earnings went to these boys' little bellies, she'd get on my case for sure.

I'm wide awake now, so I roll out of bed and pull my hair into a ponytail. "Get dressed," I tell them both, and hurry out of the room to check on Mami.

***

I race down the hall of the small trailer to the kitchen. Mami is already up, preparing tortillas and warming *frijoles* from yesterday over the small, aging stovetop. We only eat black beans in our house, because that's apparently what Guatemalan people prefer. All my friends at school have parents from Mexico, and they never eat black beans. It sets us apart.

Our kitchen has those old, cracked countertops from the 1970s, and whenever Mami scrubs them really hard, I always worry that they will chip away into fragments. I squeeze into the small space beside Mami and kiss her on each cheek quickly. "*Buenos dias,* Mami." She is a few inches shorter than me, and she leans into the kisses.

"English, *mija*," she tells me. Her eyes have crinkly lines around them; she calls them her worry lines. I think she worries too much about what language everyone speaks.

"Good morning, Mami," I dutifully repeat. She smiles before turning back to the stove. Mami is working on three of the burners already, turning our scraps of food into a meal.

"Can you make the coffee?" she asks me. I nod. My job is to prepare the coffee for everyone and set the table. She will fry an egg for each of us kids and two for Papi, but never for herself. She tries to eat at mostly at work so that we save money, but she always joins us at the table for a small portion.

I fill the metal canister with water and coffee grounds and place it on the last burner of the stove, where it will slowly percolate into perfect enough coffee for all of us. Next, I set the table with a plate and mug for each person. Papi, Mami, and I have larger mugs. My two little brothers have smaller ones. I place a fork and a spoon alongside each plate and refill the napkin holder. By the time the table is set, Mami is ready for me to start carrying food to the table.

It must be hard to be Mami. She has to make sure that we have enough to eat, when really, we don't have enough money for food. I take the stack of tortillas and smash refried black beans into one of them, then fold it in half like a quesadilla. I repeat this a few more times, making two "bean tacos" for each of my brothers. I place them on their plates next to a scoop of eggs. On Papi's plate, I give him the best helping of eggs and beans, along with three rolled up tortillas. I do the same for Mami, except without the eggs. When I get to the end, I realize I've overserved everyone else. I place a thin layer of beans on two tortillas for me and set them onto my plate. Hopefully, Mami won't notice. She doesn't eat enough.

***

Next, I serve the coffee. The larger cups are filled almost to the top with coffee, and a spoonful of sugar is added to each. I stir the sugar and then add a few drops of milk. Milk prices have been rising all summer since we're in another drought. For my brothers, I fill their cups halfway with coffee, stir in some sugar, and then fill them to the top with water. They get a few extra drops of milk. They're growing; or at least, they're trying to.

Mami pulls yesterday's green salsa out of the fridge and hands it to me. I place it on the table in the middle, so that everyone can have some. As I make finishing touches, she wipes her hands on her apron before she hurries down the short hallway to bring my Papi and brothers.

"Good morning, Mami," I hear each of them squeal. The sounds of kisses and noisy little boys fill our small trailer. Papi follows behind them, already dressed for work in a t-shirt, pair of jeans, and cowboy boots.

"*Gracias*, Shayla," Papi tells me. Mom shoots him *the look*, and he corrects himself. "Thank you, Shayla," he tells me. We speak English in our home.

I bend forward and kiss his cheeks, grateful for the moment of closeness. He's been pulling away from me all summer, since I grew four inches and started to look more like a half-woman, half-girl. I'm really just an awkward, tallish, skinny Guatemalan American, only-English speaking girl. He really can keep on giving me those morning kisses, because I'm nowhere near womanhood yet.

"Going for a run?" he asks slowly. He hesitates over each word, still not confident with the sounds of the foreign letters crossing his tongue.

"Yes, Papi," I answer.

Everyone sits down around the table and prepares to eat. Mami closes her eyes for a moment and Papi says a silent prayer, followed by an "Amen." We chorus "Amen," although we never know what he prays for. I wonder if he prays in Spanish or English.

Brenden looks at me, his eyes filled with disappointment. He's tired of bean tacos. It's been a long summer, and when the school year starts next week, we all get free breakfast and lunches again. I know why he's disappointed. But he won't complain. Papi hasn't found enough work this week, and Mami doesn't make enough at the diner to support us on her own. "Add some salsa, Brenden," I say automatically.

Mami notices but doesn't say anything. What could she say?

We finish eating, perhaps too quickly. "*Buen provecho*," Papi says, and Mami allows it. It's one of the last remnants of Spanish she lets Papi tell us. Everyone echoes back, "*Buen provecho*," a phrase that means that we hope the meal was good for everyone. I can tell by the look on Esteban's face that it wasn't enough, so after I wash all the dishes and clean up, I will sneak him two dollars instead of the single dollar that I promised him so that he can go with Brenden to the store later for spicy chips.

Papi leaves first. He's going to stand with the other day laborers in front of the neighborhood lumber supply store, hoping that someone offers him work for the day. I pause, watching as Mami walks him to the doorway and hands him his lunch box. They're like this, every morning. Mami, standing beside him with a sweet smile, her left cheek bearing a dimple when she stares at him. Papi kisses her goodbye and waves to all of us. Brenden and Esteban make gagging noises when they kiss, but they're both smiling too.

"Bye, Papi!" we yell out in chorus, and Brenden runs to the doorway to stand next to Mami. They wait until they've seen him walk down the driveway from our trailer park and turn the corner before they close the door. For some reason, I linger in the living room, watching Mami and youngest brother. Esteban has escaped back to our bedroom; he knows better than to wait to go to the bathroom after me.

I watch as Mami dips her arm around Brenden's waist, holding onto him as they stare at the empty road. Then, she turns around and sees me watching them. "It's going to be a good day."

Mami's words are soothing, and I want to believe her, but the hollow feeling in my stomach makes me wonder how good of a day it really is. My legs feel restless and I know I need to run to get the anxious feeling in the to calm down.

"I'm going to get ready for my run."

"I have to work in an hour, so make it quick," she tells me. What she doesn't say is that she needs me to watch the boys; we both already know that this is my job.

"Alright," I say, before pivoting around and hurrying back to my room.

Esteban is already sitting back on his bed, staring at me when I enter the room. "You should give the money to me, you know," he says. He's grown a few inches this summer, and he wants to be treated more like a big kid. He's nine, just two years older than Brenden. Where Brenden is reckless, Esteban is careful and reliable.

"You're right," I say, reaching into the top drawer of the dresser that we share. I get the top two drawers. I pull out two dollars and give it to him, then grab my running clothes before closing the drawer. "I'll be quick, but if I take the long road, go ahead and tell Mami to go to work."

He nods. The two dollars disappears into his pockets before Brenden can see it.

"See you later," I say as I pick up my sneakers from the floor. We have one bathroom for the five of us, and it's in the hallway between our room and our parents' room. I enter the small room and lock the door so that I can change in peace.

TWO

"Mami, I'm going on my run!" I call out, and I head outside.

There's a patch of brown dirt that we consider our private space right behind our trailer. Our own little backyard. The trailer park houses only fifteen families in aging trailers. Next to us is a large farm, sprawling across several acres of desert farmland. I reach my arms upwards in my first stretch, peering across the wiry fence at Mr. Sanchez's expansive yard.

I bend forward to touch my toes, my entire body aching from overexertion. My long ponytail falls forward and tickles against my face as I stretch. I've been running further and faster each day, just to prepare for the new season. Now that summer is almost over, I'm ramping up for my best season yet. I need to run faster, finish stronger, and place in the top ten at our first cross country meet this school year. If I can beat the other girls, maybe I can get a scholarship.

I need a college scholarship. I can't deal with this small, arid town along the California border anymore. We're in the middle of nowhere, and everything is dry, brown, and hot. Danger lurks in every direction. Drugs are slipping across the border, and with drugs comes crime. Graffiti is starting to crop up on old buildings and walls of my high school. The border to Mexico is just down the road, and I've heard the Border Patrol helicopter circling overhead sometimes. They chase illegals.

My parents are illegal. Well, undocumented, if I'm politically correct. We've been trapped in this dreary town for as long as I can remember. They can't go too far, or they'll risk getting caught at one of the immigration checkpoints. They can't drive, or they might get pulled over for driving without a valid license.

The furthest I've ever been is on school trips, but I've never gone as far as the ocean. It's only thirty minutes away, and I have dreamed of dipping my feet into those cool, blue waves for years.

I stand back up from my stretch and stare at the window, where Mami is looking back at me. I smile back at her automatically, so that she won't see the frustration on my face. She works too hard to know how much I hate this place. She deserves so much better. I wave at her and begin to run, as fast as I can, anywhere but here.

I look away, suddenly seeing the dark bird on Mr. Sanchez's fence. A crow is perched there, its beady yellow eyes staring straight at me. We lock eyes for a moment, and then he swoops off his perch in my direction. At the last moment, just before he might collide with me, he darts to the right instead and captures a small green lizard that I hadn't even noticed. I watch as he circles back to his spot on the fence, the lizard limp in his thick beak. His dark black feathers glisten in the early morning sun.

A chill runs down my spine as the wiry bird devours its prey. The predators out here are always watching, always hungry. Crows, vultures, and coyotes. I shake my head quickly, trying to re-focus my thoughts on anything less chilling.

***

Maybe the crow spooked Mami, too, because when I glance back at her to wave goodbye, she's not in my line of sight. I shrug and start a slow jog, heading out of the trailer park and to the right. It's the opposite path that Papi takes when he first leaves the house every day. I pass the Mr. Sanchez's large property, my eyes darting across his dry pasture to the huddle of goats that are gathering by a small trough of water.

In my biology class last year, we learned that goats are excellent grazers for the mountainous terrain in Southern California. They can walk up steep ledges and clear brush better than any human can. Dried brush is dangerous around here, and we're in constant fear of forest fires. Well, we're in constant fear of everything. It's awful, but I often wish that I could live anywhere but here.

After I pass the farm, there's a long path into the mountains that I take on days like today. I never know which direction I'm going to run in until my legs hit the concrete. I let them decide; the feel of dirt under my shoes is always more comforting than asphalt or sidewalks, and most cross-country meets are through rugged terrain anyway.

I feel my lips curl into a broad smile after my I get off the main road. I've been training hard all summer, so I decide to run short sprints followed by long, slow stretches. I suck in a deep breath and launch into a sprint, running as fast as I can along the footpath. When I reach the bend where I know there's loose gravel, I slow my pace and settle into a comfortable jog.

The path predictably changes from desert brown to pale green brush intertwined with spiky tumbleweeds. I chuckle to myself, remembering the time that Brenden and Esteban collected every tumbleweed that they could find because they heard that some guy sells them on eBay to the movie industry as props. They put up a sign and sat at the front of the trailer park trying to sell a haphazard pile of tumbleweeds, much like kids on tv are shown attempting to sell lemonade.

As I barrel onward, I map out the trail in my mind. There's a fork ahead; I can take the road to the right that I always take, or perhaps the scraggly one on the left. I've only ventured down there once before, when I really had a lot on my mind and needed a good run to center myself.

When I reach the fork, my feet carry me towards the left. I run underneath a thicket of trees, just as a large brown hawk sails towards me, his wings stretched out in a magnificent span that stretches further than the length of my arm.

I duck out of the way and the bird keeps going, but I lose my footing on the unfamiliar path. I'm suddenly falling, my feet not fast enough to ground me. I stretch my arms in front of me and brace for the impact as my body lands on a large bush.

But the bush isn't sturdy enough to hold my weight, so I crash through it and hit hard against the dirt. I'm certain that my long ponytail is now covered in wayward tumbleweed spikes.

I push myself up on my wrists; they're sore but not screaming in pain. I've got scratches on the palms of my hands, and my brand-new race shirt is covered in dirt. "Stupid bird!" I call out.

The ominous creature is gone. I stand up slowly, attempting to wipe as much tan dirt off my shirt and pants as I can. I look around the trail, suddenly aware that it's changed quite a bit since my last run.

I could turn around and go home, but that smells like defeat. Instead, I place my hands defiantly on my hips and start walking again, back in the same direction I'd been traveling. My ankles feel okay, and my legs aren't too sore. Really, the scratches on my hands and my injured pride are my only injuries.

I settle for a leisurely pace, just between a slow jog and a warm-up speed. I've proven to myself that I don't know this trail, so I decide to take it easy for the rest of the run.

I round another corner and immediately hear a man's voice shouting in my direction. "*PARE!* STOP!"

Dark green uniform, green hat, and a gun aimed directly at me.

My feet abruptly follow the command and I instantly raise my hands above my head. "I'm an American!" I call out, suddenly seeing the row of men, women, and children that are scattered across the desert ground like abandoned playthings, surrounded by a half dozen Border Patrol agents. Each agent is armed and aiming their weapon in the general direction of their terrified captives.

"*Agachase!*" the man yells at me, his pistol ready. I stand still, my arms over my head. I don't understand him.

He yells it again. I stare at the officer, my heart racing in my chest. A baby is crying, but everyone else has become dreadfully silent. I don't know what to do.

"Get on the ground!" Another man yells. I immediately drop to the floor, my face scraping against the warm, dry dirt and scattered tumbleweed remnants. I accept my place on the arid desert floor, grateful that the officer didn't shoot a bullet in my head.

THREE

"*Levántense!*" the officer shouts. They've tied my hands behind my back with some sort of plastic rope thing, and their guns are still trained on our heads.

Everyone else begins to fumble around on the ground all by herself, trying to stand. The baby that was crying earlier is now screaming out of control, and I can see that she is on the ground, too small to crawl. Her mother has her hands behind her back, so she can't lift her. Only the hot, unforgiving ground will hold her now.

"*Ya, nena, levántate,*" someone beside me whispers hoarsely. I glance over at the owner of the gruff, panicking voice. It's a middle-aged woman; short, long hair in a disheveled braid. She is raised slightly on her knees, stumbling to pull herself into a crouched position. None of them have stood up easily, but some are closer to being upright than others.

I don't understand. I could probably figure out her Spanish words on a regular day, but right now, I'm terrified, and my heart is racing. It isn't that I've never heard those words before; I'm rolling them around in my brain and not making sense of them.

An officer approaches; he is suddenly standing over me and glaring down. I stare back. "You've made a mistake," I say. "I'm an American citizen."

He chuckles, then calls to his friends. "Check it out, boys. This Mexican girl thinks she can fool me because she knows a little bit of English."

A low whistle comes from behind him.

The woman closest to me, the one with the wild eyes, is shaking her head almost imperceptibly. I instantly think of my Mami.

How afraid were they when they came to America? How did they cross?

Were they in danger?

I squeeze my eyes shut. This can't be happening to me. I'm an American. I was born here. I don't even speak Spanish.

"*Levántese*," the officer above me says, kicking the steel toed edge of his boot against my leg.

My eyes fly open and I stare at him again. He has no right to kick me. "I don't know what you're telling me to do. I don't speak Spanish," I say flatly, my eyes holding steady with the officer.

He bends down and stares at me closely. His face is like mine; he is a traitor to our people. Dark hair; cut into a short buzz cut. He has dark brown eyes, bushy eyebrows, and a tattoo of a bald eagle on his neck. All-American guy. "You look like a Mexican, but you're pretty good at pretending you're not a Mexican. Border kid, I'm guessing," he says, then laughs again. "Do you know what we do to border girls?"

The men behind him laugh, too.

"Get up, *mentirosa*," he says.

Mentirosa. Liar. An insult. That word, I recognize.

I start to push myself upwards, like I saw the others doing, but another boot lands solidly on my back and pushes me back down. I whirl my face in the opposite direction, seeing another agent looming over me. He is older, heavyset. There are angry crinkles forming around his eyes, and his lips are thin and set in a straight line. "Keep this one separate from the others," the man says, lifting his boot off me.

A calloused hand reaches down and grabs my arm, yanking me upwards and into a standing position. My legs feel wobbly from the fall and from being kicked. It's the officer who stepped on me. "What is your name, border girl?"

"Shayla," I say through quivering lips. His icy stare in the middle of this hot, dry morning is enough to make me afraid for my life.

"Alright, Shayla. We'll give instructions in English and Spanish, since you proclaim that you don't speak your native tongue."

I read the name engraved on his shirt. Smith. Of course. Officer Smith. A perfect, white, forever-in-America last name. Not a first-generation citizen like me. "Thank you, Officer Smith," I say curtly.

He scowls quickly, then glances at his name lapel. "Let's round 'em up, boys!" he calls out, still holding my upper arm. His hand tightens around my arm, and I feel my hands beginning to tingle in response to my circulation being cut off.

The immigrants are set into two lines, and one officer finally picks up the wailing child. I feel my eyes fill with tears, grateful that my parents crossed before I was born. Before I would be a criminal just for standing on this land.

"I'm an American," I say again, more firmly this time. I'm staring at Officer Smith, and his fat dimpled face maintains a smirk.

"Prove it, *Mentirosa*," he says. I feel his nails digging into my skin.

And he's right, I have no proof with me. It's my morning run, and I always leave everything at home. I'm fifteen, so all I really have is my school ID anyway. There's not even a need to carry my keys with me; the boys are home waiting for me, and they always let me back in.

"Seriously. I need to go home," I say.

The man laughs heartily, then lets go of my arm. "Sure thing, *Princesa*. You're on your way back to Mexico." With that, he points to the formed lines and indicates for me to join the back of one of the lines.

I count the heads in front of me. Twenty-two. Plus, a baby. So, with me, there's two dozen captives, and only six officers. It's such an unfair fight; these people have no strength against weapons and *La Migra*.

My feet carry me forward, because my mind and heart have begun battling over irrational plots to escape and just go home.

Why in the world did I take this stupid footpath? And what would happen to me now?

FOUR

The walk back down the mountain is cumbersome. I'm at the back, behind a string of exhausted, brokenhearted men and women. Many have tears pouring down their cheeks. There was only one child in this group, and I see the baby out of the corner of my eye, in the arms of the Latino officer. The baby has been passed around, no one really wanting to hold the little "*cucaracha*," as one of the officers called her.

I cringe at the word. They literally think she's a filthy little bug. She is beautiful, even if she is covered in dirt and sporting tear-stained cheeks.

I shake my head in disbelief. We live just north of the border, and I've always known that people enter our country over these mountains. *La Migra* has always terrified me because they're always right there, at a distance. Watching. Capturing. Stealing away people's chances.

I can't imagine their suffering. I've never really thought about it before, but I've always heard how "*duro*" the journey is. How much did these people have to endure to get here, just to have their hope ripped away from them like this?

My parents never told me what brought them to America. And I never asked. Over the years, I've overheard bits and pieces of their former lives. Something terrible happened in Guatemala, and my dad has no family left. Whatever brought them here was final; brutal. I know that Mami misses her family, so there must be at least a few of her family members that survived whatever ominous thing happened.

Suddenly, I wish I'd asked them for details. I need to know, because something very, very bad is happening to me. And I don't know what to do.

"*Apurense*," the man at the front of the line says as we tread slowly down a footpath I've never taken before. This must be one of the pathways that immigrants take when they cross. No wonder there's so many Border Patrol checkpoints, if it's that easy for a group of twenty-three people to get across the mountain.

No wonder my parents have never left this place. They really, really can't.

***

The officers filled the others into the back of two large white vans. For some reason, they've actually kept me separate from all the migrants. I'm standing next to one of those white and green Border Patrol vehicles, and the Latino guy.

Officer Gomez, according to his name badge, approaches me and cuts off the plastic thing from my hands.

"Get in," he tells me, pointed towards the back seat of the SUV.

I breathe a sigh of relief. Of course. They're going to take me home. "Great, I live a few miles from here," I say.

He laughs. "No one believes your ridiculous story about being an American," he tells me. "Get in."

I straighten out my arms and rub the area where the plastic tie had been absently. "Why did you separate me?" I ask, still standing by the open door.

"Don't make this difficult," he says.

I glance behind him, seeing that the baby has ended up in the arms of a red headed officer named Officer Garrison. He is approaching us.

"Is she going to hold the baby or what?" he asks Officer Gomez.

Oh. I sigh, my shoulders dipping low, realizing that I'm just a glorified English-speaking babysitter, I turn and climb into the back seat. Once I'm in my chair and I've clasped the seat belt around me, Officer Garrison passes the baby to me.

Her face has dirt caked against it in little teary rivers. Those little dark eyes peer up at me with such a wave of sadness that I hold her against my chest instinctively. "It's okay, little one," I whisper.

"What did you say your name was?" Officer Gomez asks. He's climbed into the seat beside me. The driver climbs into the front seat. There are two guards per vehicle. The other immigrants are all tied up, and I'm the only one with free hands.

I keep my eyes trained on the frightened baby, feigning a smile for her sake. "Shayla Ruiz," I tell him. I quickly add, "I was born in El Centro."

"Sure, and I'm the Easter Bunny," he says. The engine turns on, and the driver takes up his position as the last vehicle in our small caravan. We begin moving forward, towards whatever cage *La Migra* uses to trap its prisoners.

I shrug, smoothing down the baby's hair and trying to wipe away some of the dirty tears with the edge of my t-shirt. "Alright, so you're the Easter Bunny. Can I get a Cadbury egg and a ride to my parents' house?" I ask.

"It's okay, little baby doll," I say to the infant. I can't remember the word for baby doll; it's on the tip of my tongue and it starts with an 'm.' The baby isn't even making a sound; not even a whimper. Her eyes are darting between me and the guy to my left. I've never seen a baby this quiet, this terrified. It's unnerving.

"How old is she?" the Latino officer asks me.

I turn to look at him. He looks like he could be my uncle, if I had one. Same skin, same hair color, same eyes. He could probably pass as my cousin or even my dad. But he's a traitorous Border Patrol agent, and he doesn't believe a single word I've said. "How should I know?"

"They didn't tell you when you crossed with her?"

I shake my head firmly. "I've never met her before."

"She seems awfully calm in your arms," he tells me.

I cuddle the baby even tighter, against my chest, turning her head away so that she won't have to look at this man. She lets out a tiny cry but then goes quiet again. "She's terrified," I say. "Everyone is."

"Even you?"

"No," I lie. "I'm an American, and you have to let me go."

He laughs again. His cackling startles me and sends a chill down my spine.

I pause, recalling something from the news. "Wait, why did you separate her from her mother?" I ask.

Officer Gomez's eyes are dark, probably as dark as his soul. "We can't be sure that's his mom," he says.

"But what will happen to her?" I ask. He shrugs. I think of the images of little babies being separated from their parents; of news stories where little ones end up bussed or flown to foster homes in other states. I remember staring at the news in horror and disbelief.

But here we are. "What will happen to her?" I ask again, my voice rising.

"Why, is she yours?" the man asks.

I shake my head, trying to choke back tears. "She has a Mama. Why would you take her away from her Mama?"

"That's the penalty for entering our country illegally," he says, a faraway look in his eyes. Whatever indoctrination this man had to go through to become one of them, one of the infamous *La Migra* officers who would steal a child due to blind allegiance to a system that hates our people, I don't want to be a part of it.

"*Pobrecita*," I whisper. The word Papi used to say when he saw me fall down or cut myself.

"See, you do speak Spanish," the officer taunts.

"No, I don't. I only know a few words. We only speak English in my home," I recite. Now I get it. Now I understand why they didn't want me to learn their language. This newfound knowledge hits me like a wall of bricks. *Pobrecita.*

Meanwhile, our caravan has made its way onto a two-lane highway, and we're driving away from my little town and my parents. Away from my brothers, who are surely sitting in the tiny living room in our trailer, waiting for me to come home from my morning run. Away from my high school, which is slowly waking up to reopen next week, and away from my dreams of securing a cross country college scholarship.

Away from everything I've ever known.

"Where are we going?" I ask again.

"You ask a lot of questions," the man tells me dismissively.

"I guess I'm just a typical American teen," I quip, and roll my eyes for full effect. He doesn't respond. The driver in the front seat has been watching us through the rear-view mirror, but he's silent too.

The rest of the trip, I watch as distance grows between me and my family. Wherever they're taking me, I'm starting to worry that it's going to be too far away for my parents to rescue me.

I close my eyes and feel the hot tears as they begin coursing down my cheeks. I have to be brave. I have to be strong. I can do this.

But really, I can't. I'm fifteen, and I'm terrified.

FIVE

The two vans roll through the gates first. We've driven for over an hour, and we're somewhere west of my hometown. I've been watching road signs and trying to soothe a baby that's gone silent for the better part of the past thirty minutes. We've traveled mostly down the 94 west, around curvy mountain roads and past road signs to other small hometowns for other American girls like me.

Now, we're entering what is clearly an immigration prison. The tall fences that surround the facility are wrapped with curved barbed wire at the top, and there are small buildings set up in what looks like barracks. It's the only word that comes to mind when I try to figure out my new surroundings. The border patrol officers are all dressed the same, in dark green pants, shirts, and hats. They have permanent angry scowls on their faces.

The two vans park next to two separate barracks. My driver parks in front of a different building between the barracks. I watch as he gets out and walks around to my side door while Officer Gomez sits in silence next to me. "Is this how it happens?" I ask him.

He furrows his brow. "What do you mean?"

I shrug, tracing an invisible line on the baby's cheek. "You know, when you take the babies and give them away?" I want to know. "Or are you going to give her back to her mom?"

The side door opens, and the driver is beside me, his arms scooping in to take the baby. I release her from my gentle grasp.

My arms suddenly feel weightless as he lifts her away. She erupts in screams, reminiscent of the forest floor.

She isn't mine, and I can't save her. I'm still just a kid.

But I can't stop the angry tear that escapes down my cheek. "She wants her Mama." I swipe it away with my suddenly empty hand. "And I want mine, too."

"We'll get you home soon enough, kid," the driver says. Officer Gomez is still quiet.

I watch as the driver walks into the building with his captive, a smallish, dirty, suddenly screaming again baby. And it's just me, an open car door, and Officer Gomez. "Now what?" I ask.

He sighs heavily. "Why do you speak English so well?" he asks.

"I told you already. I'm an American," I say defiantly. I cross my arms over my chest, hoping that they won't tie me up again. I'm watching the line of men and women get herded into the two different barracks in my peripheral vision. For some reason, they've kept me apart from them.

He mumbles something that I can't distinguish, then releases his own seat belt. I watch as he pushes open his door and slams it behind him. I'm still frozen in my seat, waiting for my next command.

When he walks around to my side of the SUV, I stare up at him nervously. "Can I call my mom?" I ask.

"How old did you say you were?" he asks.

"Fifteen. I'm a sophomore in high school, back in Calexico," I tell him.

He shakes his head slowly, letting out a whistle. "Right," he says. But there's something about the tone of his voice that makes me wonder if he believes me or not.

***

When they finally let me stand up, after I've watched every single one of the twenty-two men and women get frisked and escorted into their barracks, I am instructed to follow Officer Gomez into a surprising brick building.

It's weird, because there aren't a lot of brick structures out here in the desert. But someone took the time to design this building with light colored bricks and some extra archways. It's by far more ornate than the two long barracks that house the inmates, and it doesn't fit well with the harsh landscape around us. The ground is typical for the desert; it's covered with the same grey-brown dirt as my small city. But the mountains behind it are arched up in steep, jagged edges, and it's unlikely that anyone can cross over that rugged terrain. Large rocks and boulders dot the mountainside, and plant life here is limited to short shrubs and dried grasses. There are no trees.

"Come with me," Officer Gomez commands. We walk through an impressive doorway into a large office. There are cubicles set up with desks and personal effects on the left. On the right, there is a long corridor with doors along the wall.

I don't ask, but Officer Gomez notices where I'm looking. "Interrogation rooms," he tells me. "We're going to have to chat with you."

"Why?" I ask. What could they possibly need me to tell them, I wonder.

"We need info on your Coyote. Where is he?"

He's pronouncing it differently. Like "coy-oh-tay." I've heard my parents use that word before, but I've never asked what it meant in Spanish. Was it the same?

"Coy-oh-tay?" I ask nervously. The word feels strange in my mouth. Normally, when I say coyote, I'm talking about those pesky little wild animals that eat "missing cats" or "missing puppies." Everyone knows they aren't really missing; they were a coyote's dinner. Those posters, tacked to power lines and fences, fill me with a sense of melancholy. I've always dreamed of having a pet, perhaps a kitten or a puppy, and there are people who carelessly leave them out for them to be slaughtered by wild animals.

Officer Gomez meets my eyes and impatiently taps his foot. "Yes, coyotes."

"I didn't see any. I mean, there was a crow that flew right at me. Actually, there was a hawk also, what are the chances of that?" I ramble nervously. "But there haven't been any coyote sightings in my area for a few months."

The look on Officer Gomez's face makes it clear that I've answered incorrectly. His forehead is crinkled, and he is frowning at me. "Coyote," he says again, with Spanish pronunciation.

I shrug. "I really haven't seen any. I could call my coach and ask?" I suggest. "Because I don't think my parents would have seen them. All they do is work, so I don't think they go up to the mountains much."

He reminds me of one of those cartoon characters whose faces get redder and redder, until they explode with anger. But instead, he just grabs my shoulder and drags me to the first door along the hallway. He opens the door, exposing one of the small interrogation rooms that he referred to. There is a table in the center of the room, a chair on each side, and a long glass window along one wall.

"Sit," he says, releasing his grip on my shoulder and pushing me forward, just as forcefully as when he kicked me back on the mountain.

I walk the short distance to the table and sit down, just as the door slams shut. I reach down to the spot on my leg where his boot struck me and notice the large purple bruise that's formed, alongside too many small scratches and a few other bruises.

With nothing else to do but wait, I reach back and release my hair from the long ponytail and begin to rebraid it. It's a nervous habit of mine, but I tend to braid my hair tighter when I need a distraction. And boy, do I ever need a distraction.

SIX

I've braided and rebraided my hair three times already. I paced the room, looked through the obviously one-sided window and tried to imagine who is staring in at me. Perhaps thirty minutes has passed, I'm not quite sure. I'm about to start a series of stretches and perhaps rebraid my hair again when the door opens.

"Have a seat," a tall man says. Beside him stands a woman, several inches his junior. They are standing in the doorway, blocking the only exit.

I am standing between the long one-way window and the wooden table that is at the center of the room. The two officers are dressed in the same dark green outfits, but there are no names on their chests.

They have the power to let me go home. I quickly sit down and wait for whatever questions they've brought with them.

Once I'm seated, they fully enter the room and close the door. The stern woman sits across from me, and the man looms overhead. I fold my hands together and begin counting in my head.

One, two, three. They're silent.

Four, five, six, seven. The man sighs deeply.

Eight, nine, ten. "What is your name?" the woman asks.

The numbers fade away. "Shayla Ruiz," I tell her.

"*De que ciudad viene?*" asks the man.

I stare at him curiously. They really, really keep insisting that I speak Spanish. But I don't. My parents didn't teach me their language.

Eleven, twelve, thirteen. "Answer the question," the man demands.

"Shayla Ruiz," I repeat.

"*Ya, nena, no tenemos tiempo,*" he tells me.

I shrug and sit back in the chair, folding my arms over my chest. They have made a series of mistakes with me, and I can imagine how angry Mami will be. Papi too, but Mami is the one they should fear.

"I don't speak Spanish," I tell them both. "So, if you need to ask me something, I'm going to recommend that you talk to me in English." I raise my eyebrows and stare at them for good measure after I've finished. The woman sits up straight and the man bends down a little to whisper something in her ear.

"Alright, Shayla Ruiz. Where do you live?" he asks.

I smile tersely. "Calexico. I'm an American."

He doesn't return my smile. His face is set in what appears to be a permanent scowl. "Good try," he mutters. "Where were you born?" he continues.

"El Centro."

"Which member of the group is the coyote?" Again, with the coy-oh-tay.

"Coyotes are animals," I say, "Not people." But I say coyote the right way, the way I've learned it.

They both chuckle. I watch as he nudges the woman on the shoulder. She begins to question me next. "Shayla," she says, her voice decidedly softer. "Who is the person who organized your trip into the US?"

I shrug. "I've never been outside of the US."

She doesn't look pleased with my answers. "Shayla, where are your parents?" she tries again.

"Calexico."

She glances upwards at her partner. They pass an indecipherable look between them. "Fine. Let's call them," she tells me.

I nod. "Yes, let's."

She stands and the two of them retreat to the doorway. "We'll bring a phone," she says before they exit.

What else can I say? I bite my lip and choose to remain silent. I stare at the blank wall in front of me and wait for whatever comes next.

SEVEN

Thirty minutes pass. Maybe more. I've taken to doodling on the desk absently with invisible ink from my index finger. I've pretended to sketch the dry, mountainous forest where I tried to go for a run today.

I'm about to begin a second layer of finger sketches when the door opens again. The two officers return, holding a bulky cell phone.

The woman sits again, and the man hovers over her. He really is tall. He has dark hair that is trimmed short, maybe a size one on the trimmer. I know barber sizes, because cutting my brother's hair is one of my jobs.

Across from me, the woman clears her throat. "Call your mom," she says.

"What time is it?" I ask, suddenly aware that I've lost track of time in this place.

"One o'clock."

My whole life has fallen to pieces in just a few hours. I suddenly feel like this morning's breakfast was years ago. Some distant past that I'll never recover.

"In the afternoon?"

"Yes." A sick feeling burns through my stomach. My brothers must be so worried about me by now. Does Mami know I'm missing? Captured?

I nod and take the phone that she is handing me. My parents don't have cell phones. Mami will be at the diner. I slowly type in the area code and the number to my Mami's work and hold the phone to my ear.

"Lucy's Diner," Patricia says. She works with my mom and makes the best hot cocoa.

I'd give anything for a mug of Patricia's Mexican hot cocoa with marshmallows, whipped cream, and chocolate powder sprinkled on top right now. In the diner. Away from here. Home.

"Patricia, this is Shayla," I say rapidly. I don't know how long they'll let me talk. "Can I talk to Mami?"

I hear Patricia set the phone down and call for my mom, then the sound of the my Mami's voice fills my ear. "Mami?" I ask, choking back a sob. I miss her so much, and it's only been a few hours.

"Shayla, where are you?" she demands. "Your brothers said you didn't make it home yet."

"Mami, I took a different running trail and I made a mistake. I ran right into an immigration raid," I tell her. "They grabbed me, and they keep talking to me in Spanish and I don't understand anything they're saying to me." My words run together as tears begin streaming down my cheeks. Mami will fix this. She's the smartest woman I know.

Mami is silent for a moment, perhaps developing her master plan. "Border Patrol has you?" she asks. I cry harder. It's her biggest fear. I ran right into her biggest fear, and now it's my personal nightmare.

I glance up at the two officers then, realizing that our moment is far from private. "Yes," I answer.

"*Ay, Miel*," Mami says. "What do I need to do to come get you?"

"I'll ask." I hold the phone against my chest and stare at the woman. "My Mami wants me to go home. What does she need to do?"

The officer takes the phone. "Hello, Ms. Ruiz?" she asks. Mami must've answered, because she continues. "Your daughter is claiming to be a US citizen. Are you sure that she's a citizen?"

The man looks perplexed as he and I both watch the woman engage my mom in a conversation. "Alright. And you're a citizen, too, I presume?" she asks.

Oh, no. My jaw drops.

My parents can't come for me. I know it the moment that she asks the question. "Let me talk to my mom," I demand, immediately holding out my hand.

The woman raises an eyebrow but surprises me by handing me the phone again. "Mami, I'll be okay. You stay there. I'll figure this out," I say rapidly.

Mami is crying on the other end. "Shayla, how?" she asks. "Where will they take you? They've been keeping kids in detention centers," she tells me.

I sigh. "I don't know, Mami." I squeeze my eyes shut and try to figure out if even one of my parents' friends is legal. But I can't think of any of them. Everyone in the trailer park is undocumented. Her boss is legal, but he creeps me out. I wouldn't want to ride alone in a car with him.

"Tell them that you're Mexican," Mami says. I shake my head suddenly.

"No, Mami."

"It's okay, we'll find someone to cross you," she promises. "Don't let them send you to a detention center. They might send you far away, like those kids on the news." It's been a nightmare that my parents can't tear their eyes away from; watching parents lose the very children they've traveled hundreds or sometimes thousands of miles to save. Several of the kids in US custody have died in deplorable conditions, and the news reporters have been covering the story quite a bit on the Spanish broadcast. Mami has to turn it off sometimes to keep herself from crying. I can barely understand the news when it's on, but Mami usually tells us the highlights while we do chores alongside her.

"Mami," I begin. But I don't finish my sentence. What could I tell her, especially with these two officers beside me? I'm scared? I'm fifteen? I don't have any money or ID? I don't speak Spanish? My family is from Guatemala, but I've never met any of them outside of our little family? She knows all those things.

"You're strong, Shayla. Call me later," Mami tells me, just as the border patrol officer takes the phone from my hands. When she lifts it back to her ear, Mami has already hung up.

I collapse my head into my hands and sob hysterically. My parents can't come for me. My Mami wants me to go to Mexico. I am fifteen. All those things jumble into a river of tears that flow down my cheeks.

When I finally regain my composure, I see that both officers are still staring at me. They haven't figured out what to do with me, just as much as I haven't figured out how to get home.

"Fine, take me back to Mexico," I say. Mami will figure this out. She is the smartest, bravest woman I've ever known. She knows what she's doing; she has to. I'm just a kid.

The woman smirks, and the guy lets out a little laugh. "Next you're going to speak fluently in Spanish," he says.

I shrug, swatting away my tears with balled up hands. "I'm full of surprises today," I tell them, my voice shaky. I don't think I can be as strong as Mami thinks I am.

"Alright. We'll fingerprint you and take you on the next bus."

EIGHT

The ride to Mexico is both short and silent. I'm on a large bus with darkened windows, seated in the aisle chair. There are three women per seat, and I feel the heat rising off the bodies of the women next to me and around me.

It shocks me that there are so many of us that they can pack us like sardines on a deportation bus. I've seen these buses throughout my childhood, and always felt that tug of fear that my parents will someday be taken from me.

I never, ever, even once thought that I would find my way onto one of these buses.

Why would I? I'm a US citizen with a legitimate birth certificate. I was born here. They can't deport me!

But it turns out, they can. And they have. And now I'm going to a country where I know no one. Where I don't speak the language. Where I wasn't born.

They believed my lie far easier than they were willing to accept my truth.

My hands are captured in tight handcuffs again and resting on my lap. I'm still wearing my running clothes, although by now they're not only dirty, but also grimy from sweat.

.

The bus winds around long, dirt roads. Frightened silence hovers in the air. I'm relieved that no one is talking; I don't know enough Spanish to understand much of what they say anyway. It'll just shoot my anxiety through the roof at this point.

As I peer sideways and glance towards the front of the bus, I realize something.

There are no children on this bus.

I wonder about the baby.

I don't know if she's still with her Mama, or if they've been permanently separated.

I suddenly think I understand what Mama was worried about. It would've been impossible to get home from a detention center.

After all, it can't be too hard to cross back into the US.

Right?

NINE

I've lived at the edge of two countries my whole life. When the bus crosses the threshold between the US and Mexico border and delivers us without fanfare to the other side, I start shivering.

I'm not cold. We're in the middle of a record heat wave and we haven't seen real rain since I was a little kid.

No, I'm not shivering from the weather. I'm terrified.

My heart is pounding a mile a minute. Women around me have started whimpering and whispering harsh words in Spanish. I don't understand.

I want to stand up and scream, "There's been a mistake!"

But I have shackles on my feet, so I'm tied up in two places.

And, Mami knows what she's doing. I hope.

The bus slowly deboards and each person is unleashed from their chains. I stare at the officer as he undoes my handcuffs. Young, Latino. Dark hair, dark eyes. His name tag screams of a Latino surname also.

"I'm not supposed to be here," I whisper.

"What?" he responds.

Right. I can't possibly speak only English and be deported. "Never mind," I mutter as the handcuffs are unlatched. "I'll figure it out."

He pauses and looks at me for a moment, a quizzical look in his eyes. What does he see, I wonder? Does he see a fifteen-year-old American girl? Or a supposed adult who he's just exiled from her own country?

He says something else to me in Spanish, and I flinch as I pull my hands away. I don't speak this language. I wish I could understand, but I don't.

The women are starting to walk away from the border checkpoint. I watch as a long line of tired, heartbroken women begins to move slowly away. Shoulders down, whispers amongst each other as they walk down the steep hill along the border.

"What city are we in?" I ask the officer finally.

"Tijuana," he answers, still staring at me.

I nod slowly. There is a winding road in front of me, and if I turn my head in either direction, I see the tall fence that is meant to keep me out of my own country.

My coach always has us practice slow, deep breaths before we start our warm-up activities. I inhale a long, slow breath, hoping to calm my fluttering heart. Instead, I start gasping for air and let out a wheezy, choking sound. "Right."

"*Cuídate,*" the man says. That's a word I understand, because Papi says it sometimes. But instead of nodding, my eyes fill with tears.

I won't see him tonight when he gets home from work. I won't be home for dinner, or to fight over who gets to brush their teeth first in the bathroom.

I bat my eyelashes a few times to stave off a river of tears, then ask one more question. I'm absently massaging my wrists where the handcuffs had dug into them for hours. "Which way is Calexico?"

"You mean, Mexicali?"

"Right."

He points his left arm outwards, and I nod again. "Okay." Mami taught me to always show appreciation and thank my elders, but I can't bring myself to thank this man for dumping me in a country I don't know.

I shrug and turn towards Calexico. There's only one choice, so I start walking. It's up to me to find my way back home.

PART TWO
MEXICO
BORDER

TEN

"*Hola, chica,*" a man says as he catches up with me. I've been walking along the border fence for several hours, and the desert heat is bearing down on me.

"English," I mutter, not even glancing in his direction.

"You... want... work?"

I cast him a sidelong glance. Loose fitting shirt, baggy jeans. Sunglasses, baseball cap.

"Nah, I'm good," I say, picking up the pace as I walk.

"Dance?" he tries again. His hand reaches for my arm, but I duck away just in time.

I don't like how close he is to me, and I'm literally dressed for a run. I haven't stretched and my body is sore from being cramped on the bus and then walking since I was dropped off, but I instantly break into a run.

At first, he tries to keep pace beside me, but I'm fast. I've been practicing all summer, and I've got my eyes on a college scholarship, after all. Sore or not, I was born to run.

The air on this side of the border is thicker, filled with a musty smoke that is a mixture of diesel fuel and wood fire stoves. My lungs heave that new air in and out, but I don't stop running. I race down the long winding roadway and duck into a tiny corner store after I'm sure I've lost him. I hover in the aisles, pretending to examine prices while I wait. He passes by and keeps going.

I wait as long as I can before the man at the cash register approaches me and says something I don't understand. I shrug, hoping that my lack of Spanish isn't written across my face. I walk outside slowly, terrified that the man who wanted me to "dance" for him might still be out here. Looking for me.

"*Hola, nena*," a girl's voice says.

I turn to the direction of her words. She's a little older than me, dressed in a skimpy spaghetti strapped dress and full makeup. Her eyes look tired. She says something again, and I shake my head.

"*Inglés*?"

I nod.

"*Me llamo* Cara," she says. "*La Migra*… deport you?"

"Yes," I whisper.

"*No estás*… safe. You need *crucer en Tecate*."

"*Tecate*?"

Cara points in the same direction I've been traveling; parallel to the border. "Hungry?"

I don't know if I should trust her completely, because I don't know why she'd be so nice to me for no reason at all. I'm just a spoiled American kid who doesn't speak my native tongue. But for some reason, I want to trust her.

"Come with me. *Te compro tacos.*"

I don't have a lot of options, so I follow Cara to a taco stand half a block away. She buys us each a plate of three *carne asada* tacos and a glass bottle of soda.

She continues speaking to me in a strange combo of Spanish and English, so I figure out most of what she's trying to tell me while we eat.

"*No estás* safe. They take *nenas* here," she tells me while she squeezes half a lime over her tacos. "Traffic. *Tienes que salir. Ahora, nena. No estás* safe."

"Oh," I whisper in between small bites. My thin bean taco breakfast seems like it was weeks ago, but even so, I'm not that hungry. Fear has won over, and I feel so nervous I might vomit.

"Go East. *Allí,*" Cara tells me when we're finished, pointing along the border wall. She hands me a few crumbled bills. I glance at them, surprised by the large numbers on them. "*Pesos.*" She's given me two hundred pesos, and I don't know how many dollars they are but it's so much more than I had before she found me.

"*Gracias,*" I whisper.

She leans in and gives me a solid hug before we part ways, the scent of sweat and aerosol hairspray lingering on me long after she scurries away. I watch her body disappear down the road before I hurry back in my opposite direction. I've got a long way to travel, and the sky has already begun to darken.

ELEVEN

The first night is the hardest. It's hard to believe that California is just on the other side of the fence, and somewhere not too far from where I'm standing, there are small families like mine. Sitting together at dinner, talking about how their days went. Sharing a warm meal inside the four walls that protect them.

I would give anything for four walls.

Instead, I find a dark corner to hide in behind a dumpster. I don't want to run into any other scary men who traffic young women.

I don't want to know learn the secrets that Cara carried away with her when she walked back to wherever she came from. Even though I only met her for a quick afternoon meal, I'm worried about her. I'm worried about her, other girls like her, and mostly, me.

I don't want to be forced into something I barely understand.

The stench from the dumpster makes the tacos twist and turn in my stomach. But fear holds me firmly in my hiding place for the entire night. The soft pitter patter and squeaking noises of rats awakens me in the morning; my back sore against the stained concrete wall behind me. The beginnings of daylight have arrived, and I won't stay here.

I stand and try to brush away the acrid scent of the crevice where I spent the night. But it follows me, even as I begin walking the odor lingers. I feel like I'll never be clean again. Or warm. Or safe.

That feeling motivates me to keep walking. Keep moving. Avoid eye contact, avoid conversations.

I train my eyes to look for road signs that say Tecate. The measurements are all in kilometers, so all I really know is that I'm getting closer. I don't remember the conversion equation for miles and kilometers, but I think my cross-country coach once told us that a 5-kilometer race is something like 3 miles. 49 kilometers becomes 40, then 25, then 8. I know I'm making progress.

I walk during the day, hide at night. I hand over the smallest number of pesos that I can for bread, because I only have the money that Cara gave me, and it's almost gone.

If I wasn't so exhausted, I'd just run the last 8 kilometers. But there's a part of me that is worried about what will happen when I get to Tecate. Because I have no idea how or where to look for a coyote, and that's my ticket home.

TWELVE

Night is approaching fast, and I'm just as lost but in a new city. Last night was terrifying, and I have no money or way to call my parents. They must be worried sick about me.

"I'll find my way home," I whisper into the hot, evening air.

I wander slowly, trying not to stand out. My skin lets me blend in, but my dirty tracksuit makes me stand out.

Not to mention what happens when someone talks to me.

I don't understand anything that people are saying.

There is a small park a few blocks away, and I can see a few small benches. I walk towards it, trying not to go too fast because that might attract attention. I dart my eyes around from left to right, constantly scanning, constantly making sure that no one is following me.

Whereas Tijuana was filled to the brim with people trying to find their way across, this smallish town is different. There's a false sense of calm that makes me want to cry or scream or run. Mostly run. Usually, when I feel this tense, I put on my running shoes and race around the dirt roads and mountainside near my parents' home.

I can't do that here.

I stroll past "*mercados*" and "*farmacias*" and a bunch of other small businesses. At least those are some of the words I know. Those are the words that I've seen hanging in local businesses since I was little.

When I finally arrive at the park, I'm glad to see that it's empty. There aren't any other people occupying those benches that I've been hoping for.

I walk past the first bench and make my way over to a lonely bench in the middle of the park. There's a strange line of graffiti spray painted across a stone bench, and I can't quite decipher it.

"*Ay, Mami*," I whisper softly as I lean against the seat. "I wish you'd taught me Spanish."

The trees around me are dry and thin. I'm still close enough to home, and the plant life is recognizable. I spend a long time watching a small grey lizard skittering around on the trunk of a nearby tree.

"*Hola*," says a man's voice from somewhere behind me.

How did someone sneak up on me? Again?

I stand abruptly, turning my head to face a heavily tattooed man. He's muscular, but not too much taller than me. Our eyes lock, and I shiver in spite of the heat.

"*¿Estás bien, chica?*" he asks.

I don't speak. I can't. If I open my mouth, this tattooed, strong looking guy will know that I don't fit in here.

"*No me hablas?*"

He approaches me and we're suddenly only a few feet apart. I can see beads of sweat trailing down his arms. Even in the early evening, the summer heat remains heavy in the air.

"*Estás muda?*"

I shrug. I don't know what he's saying, but I can only imagine. He probably sees right through me. I'm lost and he's here to tell me where I belong. Like the guy in Tijuana who aimed to make me into a dancer. I shudder at the thought.

We stand like that for several minutes, staring at each other. I'm holding my arms tightly across my chest, waiting him out. He'll lose interest, I hope.

But he doesn't. He sits down on the bench next to me and stretches his arms. I stare at him, even though I know I should look away. "*Siéntate*," he tells me, gesturing to the seat beside him.

I sway sideways a little on my feet. I figure out that he's telling me to sit, but I don't want to be in such a close space with this man.

"*Cómo te llamas?*" he asks.

I turn away for a moment, trying to think. The lizard leaps off the tree and scurries away in the grass. I can run fast like him. But I don't know where to hide.

"*Nena, oí que buscas un coyote,*" he says.

I glance back at him. "*Coyote?*" I repeat softly, hoping I pronounced the word correctly.

He smiles. "*Dime. Adónde vas?*"

I bite my lip. This conversation is getting nowhere. "Are you a coyote?" I ask, my voice barely audible.

"No Spanish?" the guy asks. He's looking at me strangely. I feel self-conscious with the intensity of his gaze, and nervously tuck a strand of hair behind my ear.

Finally, I shake my head. "No."

"*Bueno*," he says. "I can speak both."

"Wait, you speak English?" I ask, suddenly intrigued. He looks terrifying, but I've felt so lost all week. I weigh my choices and realize that I don't have that many options.

"Sit down, *nena*," he tells me calmly. Like he's spoken to many lost girls like me before.

I don't want to sit just because he tells me to, but there's something about the way that he's looking at me that makes me feel like he's not planning to hurt me. I sit at the far edge of the bench and turn my body slightly to face him. "You're a *coyote*?" I ask. I can hear the fear in my own words.

He smiles broadly. "Yeah," he answers. "Trying to cross?"

I nod. "I need to go home."

"Deported?" he asks.

"Yes."

He rests his arm on the back of the bench and stares at me. His gaze makes me uncomfortable and I look away. I don't see the lizard anymore.

"Where do you need to go?" he asks.

I cross my legs at the ankles and try to sit as still as possible. Like a lizard, hiding in plain sight. Movement could be dangerous, or it could save my life. "Calexico," I whisper.

His eyes make my face feel warm and prickly. My fingers move automatically to my cheek, where I try to smooth away the tingly sensation from being inspected so closely. He laughs. It's a slow, deep chuckle with a hint of menace.

I glance back at him. He smiles. "Three thousand dollars."

He's the only *coyote* I've found, and that's a lot of money. Probably more than my parents can afford.

But it's not like I have a whole lot of options right now. And he speaks English.

"Okay."

He fishes a cell phone out of his pocket. "Let's call your family."

***

"Mami?"

"Ay, *Dios mio*, we've been waiting to hear from you all week!" Mami screams into the phone.

I glance at my coyote, who is watching me closely from his spot beside me on the bench. "It was a long walk from Tijuana. I had to hitchhike a little."

"Where are you?"

"Tecate."

"You're close. You just have to get across the border," Mami says.

"Right. I found a *coyote*."

There's a pause for a moment, then I hear my Papi's voice. "Tell him we'll pay whatever he's asking."

I bite my lip harshly. "He wants three thousand dollars."

"Fine. Tell him we'll pay."

"Okay," I say.

The coyote nods. "Let me talk to him," he says. And immediately takes the phone from my hand and switches to Spanish.

I don't know what they're saying, and I don't like it. At the end of the conversation, the *coyote* asks him in English, "How long do you need to come up with the money?"

"Mmm."

I can't hear my Papi's answer. The coyote has his phone smashed right up against his ear.

"Right. I've got a house in town. I'll get her fed and cleaned up. I'll cross with her when you have the money."

I wrap my arms over my chest. I'm supposed to stay with him?

I guess I hadn't really thought this through. Where else would I stay?

"Lista?" he asks me, sending me an obnoxious wink. I don't say anything, so he translates. "Ready to go to my house, Shayla?"

My Papi must've mentioned my name to him. I sigh, and my shoulders involuntarily slump a little lower. "Yeah. But, um, do I call you *Coyote?*"

He laughs. "Josue." He sticks out a hand for me to shake. I ponder it for a moment. "I'm a businessman," he says.

I guess it would be rude to refuse his hand, so I reach out and place my hand against his. His grip is stronger and firmer than I expected. I stare at the tattoos on his arm, seeing a jumble of ink. "Let's go," he says, releasing my hand.

"Okay."

THIRTEEN

Josue's house isn't too far from the park. At first, we walk down a crumbling sidewalk, then he points out a beat-up old car. I wonder if he wants the three thousand dollars to replace this piece of junk.

"Get in," he commands after he unlatches the passenger door.

I've already figured out that he holds all the power in this arrangement. I lower myself into the car and lean back against the rickety car seat. It's old and I can feel at least three springs poking against my back, but it feels amazing after all the walking and awkward attempts at sleep I've had over the past week.

I've spent so much time in my own head since I ended up here that I don't even try to start a conversation. I just watch as Josue shifts between gears and navigates us along old asphalt roads. Up a hill, then down, then around a bend. He turns sharply to the right and guides us down a narrow dirt road before an old house comes into view. There's a tall, cinderblock fence built around it, and the house itself is single story. He stops the car at a gate and jumps out to unlatch it.

I remain quiet as he pulls the car inside the gate, then hops out to lock us in. He saunters back slowly, then retrieves his keys almost as an afterthought.

"Getting out?" he asks, a chuckle following his words.

I feel like I'm snapping out of a trance. I'm suddenly locked inside a cinder block fortress with a man I've just met.

And I don't like it.

I realize I hadn't put on a seatbelt. How quickly customs fall to the wayside. He's at my door already, holding it open and peering down at me. The tiniest hairs on my arms stand on alert.

I climb out of the car and stare up at this taller man who holds all the power because he speaks both languages and knows how to cross. I think this is the moment when I'm supposed to have a scary "don't mess with me" look on my face, but I don't really know how to do that. I've always been the cheerful, smiling type.

So instead, I raise one hand over my eyes like a sun shield, even though the sun is dripping down behind the mountains already.

"Is there anyone else here?"

"Not yet. I'll see if anyone else plans to cross," he tells me. "I prefer to take a few people at a time. To make it worth the risk."

"Oh."

I realize two things. I'm probably just a business to him. And I guess he could afford to repair the car if he wanted to. Or even replace it.

"Look, I get it that you're nervous. But I'm tired and it's dinner time. Let's go in, okay? You can do that nervous girl thing later."

I nod. What choice do I have, right?

And apparently, he's used to girls being terrified around him.

I fold my arms over my chest and follow him inside.

FOURTEEN

"So, you didn't bring anything else to wear?"

I glare at him. We're seated at a small wooden table in the kitchen, and he has served me two quesadillas. He fired up his stove quickly when we got here, and I was instantly grateful that he didn't expect me to cook for him.

"No. I didn't plan to get deported."

"Right. So, tell me something. Where were you born?"

"California."

"Baja?"

"What's that?"

"Baja California. You know, here in Mexico."

I shake my head, suddenly afraid. "Um. I'm an American citizen." I watch as his eyes widen.

"Why do you need a coyote, then?" he asks.

I shrug. "Personal reasons."

"Mmm-hmm. I've heard that before."

I don't answer him. Instead, I take a bite of my quesadilla and decide it isn't awful. I don't want to know too much about this man.

***

I can't sleep.

I feel more restless than I felt before All-States last year. The coach let me run in the qualifying race, and I placed twenty-sixth overall in the state. Number one for my school.

That same nervous energy is flowing through me.

I climb out of bed and lace my shoes. When I walk into the living room, I see that Josue has camped out on the sofa. He was kind enough to let me sleep on his bed. And even kinder to not bother me while I slept.

I'd kept an eye open for half the night just in case he tried anything.

He opens his eyes and stares at me wordlessly.

"I need to run," I tell Josue.   There's a weird energy flowing through me that I just can't explain. I'm unsettled. Terrified of everything and the only way to release the fear is to run free. I've been feeling trapped ever since the gate closed behind us yesterday. If I'm honest, ever since I was first arrested by *La Migra* back home.

"*Qué?*"

"Run. Like, exercise."

"*Ay, nena*. It's too early." I watch as he rubs the sleepiness away from his eyes, then focuses his gaze on me.

Almost as if on command, a rooster calls out somewhere in the distance. The world is waking up.

"I don't know where I am," I tell him.

He sighs, then sits up. I watch as he stretches his arms. He's wearing just a pair of shorts and one of those white tank top undershirts that my Papi wears all the time. I can see now that the tattoos span all the way up his arms and over his shoulders. "Can't you just run laps around the house?"

"I'm not a little kid."

Josue narrows his eyes in my direction. I hadn't noticed how dark his eyes were until that moment. "Really? And just how old are you?"

I turn away and stare at his sparse walls. He hasn't put up many decorations. There's not a single photograph, just a lone aged print of a Frida Kahlo painting. Only, it's been modified, and she's wearing army fatigues and holding a gun. Her face peers back at me. The print isn't framed, and it's frayed at the edges. This house doesn't feel at all like a home.

"Fifteen," I say softly.

"Good thing I asked for three thousand," he mutters. But he puts on his shoes anyway, then stands. I watch as he fumbles with his jeans from yesterday, then pulls his keys out of them.

He shoves his keys into his pocket and moves slowly towards the door.

***

Outside of his strange, hidden fortress, I feel my body come alive again. My arms and legs are understandably sore from the walk, so I settle into a gentle jog.

Josue runs beside me, heaving in deep breaths. I try not to smile, but it's almost too perfect that I'm more in shape then him. I may just need to use this special skill of mine to get away from him. If he tries anything.

We run up a hill dotted with old buildings that are probably apartments or townhomes. Cars are jammed into every inch of available curbside space along the road. No one else is out yet, and the beginning of daylight peaks over the mountains that separate us from the United States. The same mountains I've used as my guide to find my way here from Tijuana.

"Are we... almost... done?" my running partner pants out when we reach the top of the hill.

I shrug innocently and turn to the right. He matches my slow pace as we jog down the hill, past small houses with tiny chain-linked fences and some taller cinder block walls that block our view of the landscape inside. Branches from what I immediately recognize is an orange tree dangle over the nearest fence. But we're here, in a land of poverty, and even though I know oranges are in season, I do not see any fresh fruit hanging from the tree.

The asphalt curls upward and splits apart in places, and I narrowly dodge a pothole as we run. Josue had correctly moved me off the sidewalk when we'd started our run, since the sidewalk is worse. But the roads are in dire need of repairs.

I approach an intersection and I'm about to enter the roadway when an arm suddenly grabs my arm and pulls me to a full stop.

Just as a large, rickety box truck lumbers past us.

I hadn't seen it.

"*Cuidado*!" Josue lectures me automatically. "You aren't in the US, *nena*. You have to really, really look both ways."

My heart is thudding to its own 5k race in my chest. I glance over at him, not sure if I should thank him or ask him to let go of my arm.

He must sense my discomfort, because he suddenly releases his firm grip.

Suddenly, I don't want to run anymore. I was wrong about something. He's faster and stronger than he looks. And his eyes see everything, when mine only see what's right in front of me.

"We should go back to the house," I say, my words hollow and childlike as they spill out into the small space between us.

"Good."

FIFTEEN

Four days pass, and we've stayed inside most of the time. Josue left a few times to look for more customers, but each time came back alone.

Tonight, he brought a case of beer with him, and he's sitting on the reclining chair in his living room watching a soccer tournament with a Spanish announcer. He's working his way through his fourth beer when I glance up at him from my safe space at his tiny dining room table. I've been mesmerized by the militant version of Frida for the better part of the day.

But now, I'm curious. I stand and walk across the short distance between the dining area and the sofa beside him. It's all contained in one small room, anyway.

"I have a question," I say quietly.

Josue turns to look at me. His eyes are a little glossy, and I can tell he's working his way into getting drunk. He stares at me, waiting.

"When do we cross?"

He shrugs, then takes another long pull from the drink before setting another empty glass bottle on the ground next to him. "Do your parents have the money already?"

There is no way my parents have collected three thousand dollars already. Literally, no way. We barely come up with our monthly rent for the trailer.

But if I tell him that, what will happen to me?

Instead, I don't answer. We stare at each other for a long time, and then he takes out his cell phone. He presses a series of keys, and it dawns on me that he's already stored my parents' number in his cell.

He stretches his hand in my direction, handing me the phone. I quickly grab it and place it against my ear.

"Shayla?" my Mami pleads into the phone.

"Mami?"

"Oh, honey. We have been worried sick over you. Are you okay? Are you safe?" Mami asks quickly.

I glance back at Josue. His eyes are dark, but with tiny flecks of brown when the light hits them. He is watching me closely, waiting to hear the right words.

"Yes. Yes. My coyote wants to know if you have the money," I blurt out. I've seen enough ransom scenes on television to know that he could yank the phone out of my hands at any moment.

But he hasn't moved.

"Not yet. Papi is asking everyone. Soon."

"Oh."

My expression must have changed, because I see Josue's eyes narrow. "I love you, Mami."

"We'll get it soon. I love you, Shayla," Mami promises.

I hang up the phone call. I suddenly can't bear to hear her voice anymore, so I end the call before Josue can end it.

He's still staring at me.

"Well?"

I hand the phone back to him and shake my head. My eyes are suddenly heavy with tears, and I don't know what to do. "Not yet. Soon."

"Do you have grandparents? Aunts? Uncles?"

I shake my head again. "It's always just been my parents, me, and my little brothers."

"Interesting."

I want to scream at this man. Why in the world is it interesting that I'm practically alone in the world?

"How so?"

"Where are they from?" Josue asks. He's no more than two feet away from me, and the hairs on my arms stand on alert. My eyes dart back to the large gun in Frida's arms on his wall. This man could hurt me, and my family would be powerless to stop him.

"Guatemala."

"Hmm." He reaches down and grabs another beer, snapping off the metal cap with a bottle opener on his keychain. "Okay."

I'm not sure what he means, so I turn my attention to the television. It's safer to stare at soccer players running across the tiny screen than to keep talking to my coyote.

More than anything, I don't want to be sitting in this strange guy's house in Tecate, Mexico. I want to be home with my family, getting ready for my first day of tenth grade. Which would have been this morning.

***

A few more quiet days pass. I spend most of the day sitting on the sofa, trying not to irritate my Coyote. He mostly avoids me or goes out for a few hours to look for other migrants.

He returns alone. Again.

I've been asking him when we will cross for days, and he's been waiting for more people to cross. More three thousand-dollar payouts. But so far, it's only me.

This afternoon, he sat down next to me and guzzled a few cans of beer before taking a nap. When he woke up, he said one word to me. "Tonight."

We're going tonight?

He falls back asleep. I'm too anxious to rest, so I take a shower and re-braid my hair. I wander into the kitchen and search for something to cook, but Josue is suddenly awake and standing behind me.

"*Qué pasa?*"

I don't answer. I know that phrase, but I wait anyway.

"What's up, Shayla? Hungry?"

"A little."

"Okay. I'll cook something."

I shrink away from the almost-empty cabinets and watch as he pulls out a can of brown beans and searches in the refrigerator for something to make.

"Should I help?" I offer.

"I've got it," he says, not looking in my direction.

The kitchen suddenly feels too small for two people, so I slip away into the living room. I sit back on the sofa again, just passing time.

I should be in school. I should be home. I shouldn't be in Mexico.

And after tonight, that will all change.

I wish I wasn't so worried, but I'm starting to get that bad feeling again.

SIXTEEN

"*Lista?*" Josue asks.

I glance over at this strange man who I barely met, sizing him up one last time before our journey. "Yes, I'm ready." He is staring at me intently.

His dark eyes are piercing into me; I feel my heart thudding faster in my chest. Something about this man has me on edge, but what other choice do I have?

"Then let's go," he says.

I nod slowly. I have no backpack or belongings to gather. It's just me, in my track pants and that same cross-country shirt that I was wearing last week when *La Migra* grabbed me. I smooth the wrinkles out of my shirt, pausing for a moment. At least it's clean. Josue even lent me an outfit while I washed my clothes at his house. There's the faintest hint of brown along the edge where I'd fallen. Not every stain can be rinsed away.

He's still looking at me. "Why don't you speak Spanish?" he asks. His eyes have softened a little, and I feel my heart rate slowing down. He doesn't seem too dangerous. Just a little rough around the edges.

But aren't we all?

"Something happened to my parents in their country," I hear myself saying. "I don't really know; they won't tell me. But they don't have papers, and they were trying to prevent me from ever being singled out by Border Patrol."

He chuckles. "A lot of good that did for you," he muses.

I shake my head sadly. "Yeah. A lot of good that did," I repeat. I still got picked up by Border Patrol, and then I ended up in the wrong country with no way to communicate.

He starts to put on a dark jacket, still watching me. It's a bit unnerving.

"Are you cold?" he asks.

I shake my head. "No, not yet."

"But you will be. The desert dips low at night." I watch as he walks back to his closet and fishes out a dark hoodie. "This will work," he says, holding it in his outstretched hand.

I smile. "Thanks," I say as I take the jacket from him. "How thoughtful." And then I catch myself. Not this man. He isn't kind, he isn't thoughtful. He's a businessman, and he's kept me waiting here in Mexico for five whole days. Five extra days that I couldn't be at home with my Mami and Papi and my two brothers. He doesn't care about me.

He's a coyote. And I'm his package, to be delivered back to my parents for the bargain price of three thousand dollars.

And they don't have it. So, I'll have to wait, again, at his American house. Until he decides to let me go home.

I probably won't even make it back to school on time. It starts in a few days. And I haven't been running since a week ago, when *La Migra* picked me up and dumped me here.

"Let's go," he says again. I shove the jacket under my armpit and follow him outside to his small white car. Standard, old, nondescript. Perfect for a human smuggler.

He starts to drive, and I don't look at him again. Instead, I keep my eyes fixated on the roadway. On the long, narrow dirt roads lined with buildings labeled in Spanish. I don't belong here.

"I'm ready to go home," I tell him.

I'm not facing him anymore, so I can't see his face when he answers me. Darkness has started to fall anyway, and I'm not really interested in seeing his expression. Not this man, not the person who is simultaneously bringing me back home and keeping me from my family.

"*Muy pronto, nena,*" he says. "Your parents have to pay me *tres mil.*"

Right. Three thousand dollars. I understand his words because I've heard him say them before, to Mami over the phone. I can't imagine what my parents will have to do to come up with three thousand dollars.

I can't imagine that they ever will.

I bite my lip. I can't think about that right now. We're suddenly driving down a dark road, and the only thing I can see is what is illuminated by his headlights. We're close, and I'm suddenly terrified of whatever comes next.

SEVENTEEN

The border didn't look quite so empty in Tijuana, and in Tecate there was a solid fence. But now, here, in the desert... I see no fence. There is no border wall.

As we drove here, I sensed the passing of time. I even fell asleep, but I assumed it was just a brief nap. Now, looking at the dark expanse of vacant land surrounded by mountain chains, I realize that I slept longer than I'd thought.

"Let's go," he tells me gruffly. His voice is louder this time. Hoarse, with purpose.

"Is this safe?" I hear myself ask. I'm not sure why I even said those words; nothing in my life has been safe over the past few weeks. The border patrol detention center wasn't safe. Mexico hasn't been safe. This man isn't safe.

"*Si*," he says, his eyes locking with mine. There's something cold in his eyes. Something I didn't sense earlier. A chill runs down my spine, like a frozen lightning bolt.

He closes his car door, and I follow behind him. He explained to me how he does this along the drive. He keeps one vehicle on each side of the border, and he has a few dirty border patrol agents that make sure he gets across unnoticed.

"Follow me," he says. I do.

The ground is dimly illuminated by the half-moon overhead. No flashlights; just the memory of his feet following paths I can't see, against the dry, hard dirt.

We walk slowly for several minutes, his tall frame in front of me. When he pauses, I stumble into him, and he grabs my arm. "Watch it," he tells me.

Again, I see his eyes for just a moment, under the moon's light. There is something different about him. Something that I didn't notice earlier.

"When do we get to America?" I whisper.

He chuckles; a low, soft noise. "We crossed the border five minutes ago, *Preciosa*," he tells me. He's still holding my arm, and we're walking more slowly now. The dirt is stiff under my feet, and nothing feels different from when we were in Mexico. But we're back in my country. I'm almost home.

"Your parents," he says, releasing his grip on my arm, only to wrap it around my shoulder instead. "When will they have the money?"

My parents barely keep food on the table. I can't remember ever buying new clothes, except for the t-shirts that my team sometimes gets for us at cross country meets. Three thousand dollars is too much. I haven't been able to wrap my head around the number. I stop walking. There's one question that I have not yet asked this man.

"What happens if they can't come up with the money?" I ask, my voice cracking slightly. His grip on my shoulder tightens.

"You don't think they can get it?" he asks. There's something menacing in the way that he's leaning too close to me, and I can smell a trace of beer on his breath. It's bitter, and I shrink away from him. But he's holding onto me, and a thought passes through my mind. What will happen to me?

I feign a smile. I'm not sure how well he can see me under this treacherous sky. "Of course, they can," I lie. "They love me. They'll find a way." That part is true, sure, but it's just so much money.

His arm slips down from my shoulder to my waist. His movement is fast and slow, all at once. "How much further is it?" I ask, trying not to think about the weight of his hand. But it's all I can think about. I take a step away from him, and he releases his hand.

I take another step, but my legs feel wobbly. My balance is off, and I know it has everything to do with this brooding, dangerous man who is standing beside me. I feel his hand reaching after me in the darkness, so I move farther away. Fast, unsteady.

And I feel the moment that my ankle rolls outward. There's a sharp, familiar pain surging from my ankle up my leg as I buckle to the ground. My hands suddenly connect with the cold, thick mountainous dirt and stones and I brace myself for whatever is coming next. I bite my lip to stifle a scream; who knows if there's anyone else out here?

"Shayla," I hear him saying, his body looming over me as he bends down to survey the damage. A moment passes before he illuminates the ground with the light from his flashlight; just a glimpse before he turns it off again. My ankle is throbbing, and I doubt I'll be able to stand. "Why did you do that?" he wants to know.

There aren't words to describe to him how terrified I feel. I've never been away from home for more than a school day or a race. I work beside my mom at the diner. I'm always with my parents, and I've never felt so uncertain and afraid as I have since I got captured by Border Patrol.

I don't answer him. Instead, I push my body into a seated position. I test my ankle, moving it left, then right, then---

"Ow," I let out softly. He's already scooping me up off the ground, into his arms.

"You can't walk on it, and we can't stay here," he says matter-of-factly. As if he just labeled me as dumb-American-girl and decided for me that I don't know what I'm doing. I want to tell him he's wrong.

But he's right.

My world starts moving, one heavy step at a time. He's carrying me through the dark, mountainous desert towards his California house. He told me he keeps an old car at the edge of this mountain chain, and that's where he'll take me first.

I can't see anything, and everything hurts, and even worse, moving my head with his disconnected movements is making me dizzy. I finally give up fighting and rest my head against the evil man's chest.

He carries me for a long time under a dimly lit sky. When we arrive at the edge of the mountain path, I see the frame of an older car, underneath a thicket of trees. He shifts my weight just enough to position his keys in his hand and unlock the passenger door. Once open, he somehow balances my weight and the opening of the door before dropping me gently into the chair. The car is dark, and I notice that he doesn't turn on the inside lights.

"Put on your seatbelt," he tells me gruffly.

He walks around the car and sits down in the driver's seat. He starts the engine and begins to drive, his lights not turned on at first. When we reach the main road, he turns them on and merges onto an empty two-lane highway.

Finally, he asks the question that must've made him furious for the entire time he carried me. "Were you trying to escape?"

"No," I say softly. "I got scared because you touched me."

He chuckles. A soft, low sound, like a whistle coming from a caged beast. Menacing. "You scare easily, don't you?"

I look straight ahead at the lines on the pavement, trying not to think too much about his words. My eyes are trained on the little lines as long as I can keep them open, but eventually they're heavy with fatigue and I drift off to sleep.

PART THREE
US BORDER

EIGHTEEN

"Buenos días," Josue's voice catches me off guard, and I flitter my eyes open. Daylight is peeking in through the edge of the window that isn't covered by curtains. I briefly remember being carried into his house and placed in bed, but he made me take a few pain pills during the drive, and I was knocked out after that.

"Is this your house?" I ask groggily. My eyelids feel heavy, and everything around me seems fuzzy, like a fog is covering the room.

Josue sits down next to me on the bed. "Yes," he says, his voice a bit softer than last night. "How does your foot feel?"

I try to sit up, but my head is swimming. My elbows are bent, and my hands are braced against the mattress as I hover midway between sitting and lying down. "What did you give me?" I ask. I've never had anything stronger than tylenol, and whatever he gave me last night is still affecting me. My stomach flip flops.

"A pain pill. It was pretty strong," he tells me. I feel his arm sliding behind my back, setting my senses on high alert again. He lifts me into a seated position and slides a few pillows behind my back before moving out of range. He's still next to me, but not touching.

I stare at him. His eyes aren't as piercing as last night. I'm not sure what changed. Is he still mad at me for falling down?

"Are you hungry?" he asks.

I've stared at his face all week; tried to figure out what it is about this man that sets me on edge. One minute, he's eager to please; but the next minute, he's brooding and dangerous. And here I am, at his house. I wonder where we are. How far did we drive last night?

If only I hadn't injured myself. I could've stayed awake if I wasn't seething in pain. I'd wanted to watch the road and try to calculate where I was. My foot is throbbing again, but I don't want any more of whatever that pill was.

"Yes," I tell him.

"Great," he says. "I made breakfast."

I sense that he's waiting for something. It's weird. My whole childhood, I've heard stories of people being trapped in small buildings or vehicles when they're crossing the border, waiting for their families to pay for their release. Yet here I am, in his actual house, and he hasn't locked me away in a secluded room.

Maybe because I'm injured, I remind myself.

"Do you want to eat in bed or come to the dining room?" he asks finally.

I glance around the room, taking in my surroundings. This is obviously his bedroom, and I'm lying on a large mattress. Is this a Californian king? I've never seen one, but it feels larger than my parents' queen-sized bed. I feel small under a sea of blankets. They're mismatched but soft.

He has a large television across from the bed, seated atop a dresser. It's one of those massive six-drawer ones, and I wonder if he's meticulously arranged his socks and other clothes into separate drawers. My own dresser back home is tiny, and I have two drawers for me and one drawer for each of my brothers in our shared bedroom.

"The dining room?" I ask. I want to see more of the house, even if it means having him carry me to another room. The windows in his bedroom are covered with curtains and long blinds. No one can see inside, and I can't see out.

"Alright," he says. "Let me get a bandage to wrap your ankle first," he says.

He steps away, through a doorway on the right. There are three doors in this room; one is open and leads to a hallway. One is along the wall and most likely represents a closet. The door that he just went to opened into a bathroom.

There's a nightstand next to the other side of the bed, and it has a clock. It's tilted a little, but I can see the numbers on it.

9:07. Wow. I can't believe I slept so late.

I peel off the blanket to look down at my ankle. It's my right ankle, the same one I fractured at seven years old when I went to a classmate's birthday party and jumped wrong on the trampoline. Sometimes I re-injure it and it swells up for days. Right now, it's more swollen than I've seen it in a while. There's a purple bruise forming along the edge of that ball thing on the outside of my ankle, and it hurts worse than my last sprain.

"Hey," I hear Josue's voice as he walks back into the room. He's holding an ACE bandage when he approaches the bed. "Do you know how to wrap it, or should I do it for you?"

I reach out my hand for the bandage. Mami always wraps my ankle, but this man has touched me more than I'm comfortable with. "I'll do it," I say, my voice wavering as I try to sound older and braver.

He hands it to me, and I bend forward, feeling another rush of nausea as I move. "Oh," I say softly. He notices, because he takes the bandage back from my hand and begins to wrap my ankle.

I lean back against the stack of pillows and close my eyes. Everything feels heavy still, and I take a deep breath to fight the rising sensation of bile in my throat. My ankle is screaming in pain as he secures the bandage around it, and I can't wait for him to finish wrapping my foot.

When he does, I open my eyes and stare at him. He's seated at the edge of the bed, holding my foot at an angle. I wonder what he must think of me.

"Thanks," I say softly. I don't like owing this man anything. Yet, each clumsy move I make just adds to my tab.

"I'll bring your breakfast to the room, okay?" he says. I realize that he's frowning slightly, and there's something about the way he's staring at me that has my heart racing in my chest.

I don't like it.

"Okay," I nod.

NINETEEN

"Ow," I whisper, trying not to scream in pain as I step off the bed. Josue just left the room, and I am trying to stand up on my own. I had finished a whole cup of juice and a coffee. He's surprisingly a good cook, and my stomach feels stronger after a solid breakfast of scrambled eggs, beans, and tortillas.

I take a step forward, then continuing limping across the room towards the bathroom. My ankle hurts too much. I don't remember sprains being this painful, I realize as I stop halfway across the room. I'm standing on my good leg and holding my right ankle up in the air when Josue returns to the bedroom.

"What are you doing?" he asks in a startled voice.

I freeze. "I have to pee," I say quietly. This man is too skittish, too easily alarmed. He's instantly beside me, ready to scoop me up again.

I don't want him to touch me, but I have to get across the room on a bad ankle. I pause, trying to figure out my next move. But he's already standing next to me, and it's too easy to lean against him for support. "Sorry," I tell him as he catches me along my side. "It really hurts."

"Yeah. It's swollen," he confirms. His hand slides around my waist and I feel him lifting me off the ground. I curse myself for weighing so little that he can pick me up like a ragdoll.

He carries me to the bathroom and sets me down beside the toilet. "Call me when you're done," he says, quickly exiting the room and closing the door.

I use the bathroom first, and then stop myself from flushing the toilet. I need a moment to examine the room, I decide.

It's a standard master bathroom; large, complete with a bathtub and shower combo. I imagine soaking my aching foot and have to remind myself to focus. Toilet, sink, medicine cabinet. Clothing hamper. I reach across to the cabinet and open it. Just a few bottles of tylenol and cough medicine, alongside deodorant and cologne. Nothing fancy.

The sink is simple. There's a bar of soap, a toothbrush, and a razor next to it.

Razor. I tuck that piece of knowledge away. At least I know where to find it, if I need it.

"Are you okay?" Josue asks from outside the door.

"Yes," I say, reaching for the toilet handle and pressing it down. The water flushes away. "Just a minute," I tell him as I wash my hands.

After I turn off the faucet, I look at myself in the mirror for a moment. I hadn't noticed it earlier. My hair is still in the long braid from yesterday, but it's frizzy around each loop of hair, and it looks messy. My face is paler than normal, and there's dirt on the outfit that I borrowed from Josue.

"Can I come in?" he asks.

"Okay," I answer.

I've started to undo my braid when he enters, and he stands in the doorway, almost like he's entranced by the motion. I don't see a brush, so I comb through my hair with my fingers and start a new braid. A few minutes pass as I redo the braid and place the hair tie back at the end.

"You have nice hair," he says.

The hairs on the back of my neck stand up. "Thanks," I reply, casting a glance at him through the mirror. He's staring right at the mirror version of me.

"Are you ready to go back to bed?" he asks. I don't like the way that he says it, or the mischievous look in his eye.

"Should we call my parents?" I ask.

Josue's smile fades. "Yes, that's a good idea," he tells me. He reaches for me and I let him carry me again, back to the bed. He makes a great fuss about tucking me back underneath the covers. I suspect that he likes how miserably trapped I've become due to my sprain.

He pulls out a cell phone from his pocket, then dials the number. I notice that he dials that code that blocks his number, so that my parents can't call him back. "Go ahead," he tells me, handing the phone to me.

"Hello?" my mom's frantic voice beckons to me through the phone.

"Mami?" I ask, suddenly overwhelmed with grief. I miss her so much. I'll never think bad thoughts about her again, I swear to myself. "I'm back in America," I tell her.

"Where are you?" she asks.

"The coyote is keeping me at his house," I say. I'm watching Josue's eyes, and he's so close that he can hear my mom's words as she talks to me. He's already told me not to use his name when I talk to my parents.

"Are you safe?"

"I think so," I tell her. I don't believe my words, but I can't let her know what I'm beginning to suspect. Really, I should be grateful that I'm not locked in a sweltering shed somewhere on his property. Or worse, trafficked. Those girls in Tijuana terrified me when they told me about bad coyotes.

"We're trying to get the money, *mija*," Mami says. "Can he wait a few more days?"

I bite my lip. He probably can, but I don't want to. I miss them, and I want to go home so badly. Josue nods in answer to my mom's question, driving my attention back to the task at hand. "Mami, I miss you. He wants the money so I can go home."

He nods, but he has a strange look on his face, one that makes me wonder what he isn't telling me.

"We love you, Shaylita," Mami tells me. She usually reserves that name for me for when I'm sick. But she doesn't even know that I'm injured.

"I love you too. Tell everyone I'll be home soon."

Josue takes the phone and disconnects it. There's a long pause, and he's staring at me intently. Like my parents stare at each other when they're about to argue.

"It looks like you and I will be hanging out for a while," he tells me, his lips curving upward into a tiny smile. I swallow hard. Yes, it does.

I want my Mami. Sure, I miss my Papi, too, but it's my Mami that I keep thinking about. I want to go home.

"They'll get the money soon, I promise," I say. It's an echo of what I've told him all week, and we both know it.

He shrugs. "We'll see," he tells me, slipping the phone back into his pocket. He starts to walk away, and I'm not sure why I even stop him.

But I do. "Josue," the name escapes across my lips. "What if my ankle is broken?" I ask. I don't like the bruise or how much it hurts. I remember getting a large purplish bruise when I broke it many years ago. He turns to face me.

"I'll give you some more pain meds for now. You need to rest," he tells me.

I don't really want to take them, but when he returns to the room with two white pills and a cup of water, I don't have much choice. I swallow them quickly, trying not to think about that drowsy, drugged feeling from the morning.

As I'm fading off to sleep, I feel his presence next to me in the bed. I try to claw through the fog of sleep, but it's too strong and it weighs me down.

***

When I awaken, the room is darker. The lamp on his side of the bed is still on, but it's dull and doesn't provide much light. I stare at his large frame lying next to me in the bed and suddenly feel very small.

He could really hurt me.

But he hasn't.

I squeeze my eyes shut and try to block the frightening feelings that are coursing through me. I've never had a boyfriend. I've never been kissed. I don't like waking up in bed next to my coyote.

Why am I even in the same bed with him? Doesn't he do this all the time? Where does he normally keep the people that he brings into the United States?

"Hey," Josue says, his eyes fluttering open.

"Hi," I whisper back. I'm used to sleeping in the same room with my brothers, and sometimes they crawl into bed with me. But this is different. His physical presence has me on edge.

I wrap my arms around a pillow and pull it in front of me, like a barrier from him. I turn a little to face him. It's weird sharing this space. If Mami saw me, she'd scream and swat him with a broom or something.

"What grade are you in?" he asks. His question startles me. I'm not sure what he's trying to figure out about me.

"I'm supposed to be starting tenth grade," I say. "But classes started already."

He sighs. I'm not sure what else to say, so I don't. I clasp the pillow more tightly.

"You told me down in Mexico that you run?" he says. "What's that like?"

I lean my head down a little more on the pillow, diverting my eyes. "I don't know. I like it," I say. "I feel free when I run, like the world isn't weighing me down."

"But that's how *La Migra* got you," he says. "And then they took away your freedom."

"Yeah," I tell him. I glance back at him, and his eyes are peering directly at me. "I hope I can keep running when I get home, even after all this."

"*Pero…*" he pauses, then switches back to English. "But why?"

"I need to get a college scholarship," I say. "And not too many high school kids continue cross country at the college level."

"What are you going to study?" he asks. His voice sounds almost whimsical. Like he's never contemplated any of these things.

"I don't know," I confess. "What did you study?"

He shakes his head. "I didn't go to college. Didn't finish high school, actually."

We're staring across my pillow at each other. There's definitely more to this man's story, and I'm starting to wonder what grade he reached before his life turned into this. Was he always dangerous? Or was he a regular teen, with hopes and dreams? I shouldn't want to know, but I'm starting to wonder how he became the man in front of me.

"Oh," I say, not sure what the etiquette is for a conversation like the one we're having. Do I keep talking, or let the words fall away? Do I pretend to go back to sleep?

"How's your ankle?" he asks, blissfully changing the subject.

"It hurts, but not as bad," I tell him. The medicine made me feel heavy again, but not as bad this time. "How long did I sleep?"

He smiles, a boyish grin this time. "It's 2 am," he says. "I was wondering how long you'd be asleep."

I hold my wall between us and watch his face. His expression is typically stoic, like a mask. But right now, he looks younger. More at peace than I've seen before.

"How often do you do this?" I ask.

"Hmm?"

"You know, transport people across the border?" I want to know.

Those eyes just keep staring at me. It's unnerving. He reaches across and moves a strand of hair away from my eyes. The intimacy of his hand on my face feels like hot coals. I shiver after he removes his hand.

"A few times a month," he finally answers.

"Where do you usually keep them?" I need to know the answer, and I'm clutching the pillow in a death grip for what seems like an eternity before he starts to talk again.

"I have a building out back," he tells me.

That chill that I felt when I was running; the same one that chases down my spine when he looks at me or carries me, jolts down my spine. "Why did you bring me inside?" I ask quietly.

"You're different," he tells me, his lips curving upward a little. "Besides, you got hurt. You need someone to take care of you."

Oh. My. God. "But…"

I don't finish my sentence.

"It's okay, Shayla," he tells me before he yawns. "You'll get used to me."

I don't know what he means, and I'm not sure I'm ready to find out. "Josue?" I finally say. He looks like he's deep in thought, so I close my eyes and start counting. I need to fall back asleep. This man is dangerous, and I just need time to pass so my parents can bring me home.

TWENTY

I don't sleep well. I count to one hundred at least ten times before I finally fell asleep. He whispers my name after my eyes were closed, but I pretend to sleep until he finally falls asleep too.

My head hurts, my ankle hurts. I am not aging well in this man's house.

I sit up slowly, opening my eyes to look for my captor. He's sitting next to me, typing fast into his cell phone.

"*Hola, amor*," he says. I cringe.

"Hi," I reply. Steady, even tone. Like I've practiced talking to coyotes my whole life.

"Do you want to have breakfast?" he asks.

I nod slowly. He called me *amor*. I roll the word over and over in my mind. My Papi calls my Mami that. This can't be happening, I think to myself.

He stands up and walks around the bed, his arms reaching for me before I remember that I can't walk.

"Oh," I say nervously as he tucks his hands under me and lifts me up. "Bathroom first?" I plead.

"Of course," he says, holding on a little too tightly before carrying me across the room. He deposits me in the bathroom next to the toilet again.

After he leaves, I glance around. Everything's the same, except…

He took away the razor.

My shoulders fall. This man is two steps ahead of me.

After I finish and wash my hands, he opens the door and collects me. It's maddening to not be able to walk, but when I try to bear weight on my right ankle again while I am in the bathroom, it takes all my strength to not scream in pain.
I'm really starting to worry about my foot.

"Josue," I say as he carries me down the hallway. I'm dizzy again, and I've resorted to leaning my head against him to prevent me from throwing up. "I need fresh air," I tell him. What I really want is to see where I am. He tsks quietly. I'm not sure why, but that also makes me nervous.

"Alright, Shayla," he says. "After breakfast."

At the end of the hallway is a dining room. I've counted two doors on the right of the hall as he's taken me towards the dining room. Behind it, through an open archway, sits what looks like a living room. To the other side, there is another door. I'm guessing it's the kitchen.

He sits me down at an impressively large dining room table. I imagine what it would look like to sit here with my own family. My parents, my little brothers. A table big enough for all of us, with just enough food to eat. He's set the table with two plates, homemade waffles, and two cups of coffee.

"I'm going to need to go into town for groceries," he says after I've adjusted my position in the chair. I look up at him expectantly. I get to go to town? "We're out of milk."

I must look too eager, because he stifles a laugh. "No, Shayla. I'll go into town. You'll stay right here," he tells me. He watches my face and probably sees what he expected to find. "The closest neighbor is two miles away, and there's not phones or tablets or laptops. You'll wait for me here," he says.

He's used to crossing people into the US. He knows that we would do anything to get to our families, as soon as possible. For him, this is a business transaction. Of course, he's worried that I might leave. "I miss my brothers," I say instead.

I notice his expression change. His eyes are still piercing into me; the pools of brown are dancing as he watches me. He doesn't say anything. I take a slow sip of my coffee while I study his expression. "Do you have any brothers or sisters?" I finally ask.

He shakes his head, perhaps a little too quickly. He picks up his own coffee cup and begins what looks like the longest sip ever. I've struck a nerve, I can feel it.

I put down my coffee cup and rest my elbow on the table; my knuckles immediately setting up a resting place for my chin. We're in a strange staring contest, and he's still sipping from his mug.

Josue looks away first. But when his eyes dart back to face me, he feigns a smile. He finally puts down his mug, and I see that he's drained it completely. "Tell me about them," he says.

"Well, they're both in elementary school. Esteban is nine, and Brenden is seven," I begin. "Esteban is bright, but he doesn't know it yet. He's shy." I pause, smiling at the memory of his goofy grin. Was it just a few weeks ago that I made them bean tacos? I feel something burning in the back of my throat and realize that my eyes are suddenly heavy with tears. "He looks up to me, and sometimes he tries to run with me, but his little legs are shorter, and he can't keep up."

I reach for a napkin at the center of the table and start tearing at the edges. There's something therapeutic about the soft movement of the papery fabric between my fingers. I stare down at my fingers, noticing that my nails are uneven. I haven't been able to trim them short like I prefer them.

"Hey, are you okay?" Josue asks. I glance up. It is then that I realize that I'm crying.

"I miss them," I tell him again. "I want to go home."

Josue sighs heavily. "When will your parents have the money?" he asks.

Right, it's all about money. I snap out of my sadness and swipe away the tears with my shredded napkin. "Can I call them?"

"Maybe tomorrow. They said they needed more time."

He pulls out a pill bottle from his pocket and counts two white pills for me. He hands them to me. "Here, take some pain meds," he tells me.

I don't reach for them. I don't want to fall asleep again. My foot hurts, but it's not unbearable if I'm not stepping on it.

"Josue," I say, my voice a little hoarser than I expected. "I don't like the way those make me feel."

I haven't touched my breakfast. Actually, he hasn't either. I turn away, staring at the heavily curtained window. I need fresh air. Sunlight. I always run in the mornings, and suddenly I can't.

"You need to rest," he tells me. "And these pills will help." He drops them into my hand, and I stare at them. Two oval, white pills. They have little numbers carved into them.

I flatten my right foot on the ground under the table and test the tiniest bit of weight on it. An electric jolt of pain rides up my leg to my thigh. Immediately, I lift my foot back up so that it isn't touching the ground. Then, I pop both pills into my mouth and take a quick gulp of coffee to wash them down. Josue nods, his lips forming a flat line. I watch as he picks up his fork and knife to cut his waffles, and then points to mine.

I'm not a child, but I feel miserable and small as he chops my waffles into small pieces. He instructs me to eat afterwards. "Those pills are nasty on an empty stomach," he tells me.

Arguing with this man is futile. I reach for the maple syrup and drizzle a small amount over the waffles, then set it down between us. I take a bite, then pause. The waffles taste light and fluffy, like if Mami had made them. I want to stay mad at him, but I also want to eat.

I swallow quickly, chasing the waffle with another swig of coffee. "You made these?" I ask after I set the coffee cup back down. He nods. I give him a half smile, and say, "Thanks."

We sit in awkward silence, taking slow bites and working our way through our first breakfast together in America. It was different in Mexico; here I feel like a caged animal. When I finish eating, my head is already starting to feel heavy from the pills. Josue stands and picks me up. "Alright, *princesa*, time to sleep," he tells me.

I lean my head against that too familiar part of his neck and let him carry me back to his bedroom. Past the closed curtains, doorways to other rooms, and down the hall. He lays me back on the left side of the bed, propping up my ankle with a pillow before tucking me in. I'm not sure why his movements already feel so routine, but he's memorized my curves and knows just where to tuck me in.

"Don't try to walk," I hear him say as I close my eyes.

TWENTY-ONE

On my sixth day back in America, I decide that it's time to try to stand up on my foot. I glance over at Josue, and he's still sound asleep beside me in the bed.

I just can't get used to laying in bed next to a grown man. He doesn't seem to see anything wrong with it, but I don't like it.

I push the covers off of me and sit up. When I move my legs to dangle from the bed, I feel a sudden jolt of electricity from my right ankle. Maybe I'm not ready, and maybe this is going to hurt, but I have to know. Can I walk?

Left foot first, then right foot. I already feel a burning sensation in my foot, and I haven't even fully stood yet. I bite down hard on my lip, anticipating whatever pain will come next. I step forward on my left foot and swing my right foot behind it. I'm suddenly standing on both feet, and it hurts more than I expected.

"Ow!" I cry out, just as my foot begins to wobble. The pain is too much, I can't bear it. I feel myself falling, just as I hear a sudden noise behind me.

And I'm falling, yes, but Josue catches me. I'm almost used to the feel of his arms around me, and it scares me that it's predictable and somehow less frightening.

"Shayla," he says. I glance up at him. "What were you doing?"

I lean my head against his chest, not able to keep eye contact. "I think it's broken," I tell him. "It never takes this long to heal."

He doesn't move. He could easily walk two feet and place me back on the bed, but he continues holding me. Like it's his job to hold me in the middle of his bedroom. I can tell that he feels something for me, but he shouldn't. I'm fifteen. He's too many years older than me.

"Can I please get an x-ray?" I whisper, my voice suddenly feeling stuck in my throat. "I'm really worried."

His hand curls more tightly around me, and he slowly carries me back to the bed. He stares right into my eyes, even though I tried not to look at him. Even though he's too frightening and too old for me, and his eyes have been boring into me for days.

"Are you going to try to escape?" he asks. He's asked me this before, back on the mountain.

"My parents will pay you," I promise again. "I won't leave."

He nods. "Okay."

"Okay?"

There is concern etched across his face, from his furrowed brow to the way his bottom lip is turned slightly downward. After several long moments, he tells me, "I will take you to an urgent care."

I smile, perhaps the first full smile in days. "Thank you," I tell him gratefully. I'm so worried about my ankle. If it's broken, how long will I need to sit out of cross country to heal? I'll lose the whole season. And to be honest, it feels broken. The constant throbbing, the inability to bear weight. Ankle sprains never feel like this. I can usually put on an ACE bandage and power through my regular workouts.

He matches my smile, that dimple in his cheek blossoming. There's almost a boyish glint in his eye when he smiles.

Neither of us smile enough.

If this was another time, another place, and perhaps he was closer to my age, maybe things would be different. But even as soon as I think this, I know that I'm wrong. I've never liked a boy before, and I'm only feeling close to him because he's helping me get home. I would never be interested in someone like him if I hadn't been deported. If I hadn't been stuck in Mexico with no way to get home.

He's still smiling, and I realize I am not. A wave of concern crosses his face again. "What is it, Shayla?" he asks.

I know that he's afraid that I'll turn him in. But he's a coyote, and I was deported. Neither of us want to talk to the authorities at the moment. "It's probably broken," I say, focusing on a safe topic. "I don't think I'll be able to run for a while." And that is something that would take away my smile, but really, I do have a bad feeling about my foot. This feels worse than when the crow almost flew into me. And that other scary bird. What was it with me and crows?

"Let me find an ID card for you," he tells me. I don't really know what he's talking about, so I nod and wait for him. He rushes out of the room and doesn't come back for several long minutes. When he does return, he has a small plastic card in his hand.

He hands it to me. It has a face that is similar enough to mine. Maria Reyes.

"What is this?" I ask.

"ID. You're going to be an adult for the doctor's visit," he tells me.

I nod slowly, running the ID through my hands. Who is this girl? Where did he get this?

He is watching me, and he must be trying to figure me out. He laughs softly. "I keep spare IDs for the people that I cross. Don't worry. I have a lot of them," he tells me.

But how? I have no idea where someone would get "a lot" of IDs. Or why they would need them. Maria Reyes, whose birthday makes her eighteen. Lives in Los Angeles.

"Memorize the birthday," he says. I nod.

Josue finds a different shirt for me, then a jacket. He leaves the room while I change my shirt, and then returns to help carry me to the car.

I haven't been outside much. The other morning, he only let me sit on the porch. My movements have been severely limited, and I'm hoping for good news from the doctor at urgent care. When he reaches down to pick me up, I realize that I'm not even bothered by him carrying me anymore.

TWENTY-TWO

"Do you have your seat belt on?"

I was so excited to feel sunlight on my face and see the dry, brown mountainside beside his home that I forgot to put my seat belt on. He's staring at me like the child that I am. I grab the seat belt and attach it.

Josue turns the key in the ignition and begins to drive down a long, narrow dirt road. I'm finally seeing his entire property, and it's huge.

"This is all yours?" I ask him as my eyes memorize the long field that looks like it could fit a massive garden, the rows of fruit trees, the barn, and a few scattered buildings on his property. "What kinds of trees are those?"

My Mami has always dreamt of fruit trees; so much that I've adopted her dream. I would love to live on a piece of land like this, with soil waiting to be turned into a crop garden and trees reaching to the sky with their fresh blossoms and fruit.

Josue grins, but keeps his eyes on the road. He is such a careful driver, perhaps to avoid detection. That dimple of his pops up on his right cheek. "Lemons, limes, oranges, avocados, and pomegranates."

"Wow," I whisper. "That's kinda perfect."

I turn to watch the trees disappearing from our sight, and then look back at the road as we turn a corner around a small mountain. The car veers to the right and we enter a two-lane highway. Apparently, his ranch is on one of those hidden exit roads from the 94, I realize, as we pass a sign marking the tiny highway.

"Is it far to get to town?" I ask. I'm trying to keep the conversation up, but also trying not to ask too many questions. Josue appears uneasy whenever I ask too much, so I'm trying to figure out the right balance with him.

There are no cars behind or in front of us. We're in the middle of nowhere, and we're coasting along steadily through the twisty mountain roads that dot the border of Southern California. "Not too long," he tells me, his voice crisp. I'm pretty sure he doesn't trust me.

We drive in silence for several more miles. Around us, the mountains rise up on both sides of the roadway, and the large boulders that line the hills remind me so much of my hometown. Our mountains haven't been explored much, and the resources are still ripe for picking by developers. Sometimes, when I watch television shows and see the same Los Angeles mountain landscape in episode after episode, I wonder if all of Southern California used to look like the mountainside of San Diego and Imperial Counties. The short distances that I've gone for cross country meets have always shown me the same scenery.

"So, what do I tell them at the clinic?" I ask, turning back to face him.

Josue glances at me, then returns his eyes to the main road. "What is your name?" he asks me.

I pause, then tell him, "Maria Reyes."

"How old are you?"

"Eighteen."

"What is your date of birth?"

I tell him the date I've memorized.

"Great. How did you hurt yourself?"

I bite down on my lip, not sure what to say. "I fell?" I ask.

"They'll want more details," he tells me. "They'll ask you how, where? Are you in danger? Did someone hurt you?"

I nod. "Okay. Ask me again."

"How did you hurt yourself?" he asks.

"I tripped and fell when I was running."

He smiles. "Good. Very good." His eyes are focused, and he doesn't look at me as he rounds another corner. A solitary car passes us in the other direction. I see a few more in the distance. "And how did you land?"

"My ankle rolled out and then I fell."

"Great. I think you're ready," he tells me. "But of course, I'll be right there beside you."

"Okay." I didn't expect him to be anywhere else.

The roadway in front of us is changing. There's a sign for a diner a few miles up the road, and I see more cars ahead. We pass another sign that says, "Campo."

We're near Campo. I'm trying to remember how close that is to our little town on the outskirts of Calexico. I've been there once, when I had a cross country meet at their high school. Was it an hour? I don't remember.

"Josue?" I ask, suddenly nervous. His name sounds shaky when I say it. I realize that my hand is trembling a little.

We've slowed down, and we're approaching a red light. He pulls off to the side of the road and looks at me carefully.

"I think it's broken," I tell him. "I'm really scared."

"I'm sure it's fine," he tells me. "Are you ready?"

I nod, so he merges back into the roadway. There are only a few cars, and the town looks asleep. We drive past a small diner, and I wonder if someone like my Mami works there. Next, there's a gas station, followed by a bonafide main street. He keeps driving, past a post office, a police station, and a row of track houses. He finally maneuvers the car to the left down a side road and pulls into a small urgent care. There are a few other cars in the parking lot.

He turns off the car and looks at me again. I've lost count of how many times he's given me this concerned look, the one that screams don't-turn-me-in. "Ready?" he asks again.

"Yes," I tell him. I remove my seat belt and wait for him to walk around the car to carry me inside. Really, I am getting so used to him. I shouldn't be. It's been less than two weeks and my whole world revolves around this man taking care of me and getting me home.

He lifts me into his arms and nudges the car door closed with his hip. He uses a button on his keychain to latch the doors shut. I smile appreciatively and bury my head against his chest. Maria Reyes. I am Maria Reyes.

"Alright, Ms. Maria," he tells me, and he carries me to the door.

TWENTY-THREE

"How can we help you?" the receptionist asks from behind a small window. She's seated at a desk with a computer and a stack of clipboards. Her hair is perfectly curled, and she has makeup that makes her look like she belongs in a magazine photo shoot, instead of here in Campo, sitting at this tiny urgent care.

Josue answers for me. "My girlfriend fell a few days ago, and she can't walk on her foot."

"Alright, do you have her insurance card?" the woman asks.

Josue sighs. "Sorry, she doesn't have insurance. We'd like to pay cash."

The receptionist nods slowly. It isn't unusual to be uninsured, especially near the border. "Alright, just fill out these forms and bring me a copy of her ID," she tells Josue, handing him one of the clipboards. I cling to him so that he can reach for the clipboard.

Next, Josue carries me across the room and sets me down on a chair. He begins to fill out the paperwork for me. Maria Reyes. Some random fake address. Date of birth. No phone number.

I sit quietly beside him, watching his hand as it moves swiftly across the page. There's a section to write down what happened, and he fills it in with the most basic storyline. He's leaving room for me to say whatever comes to mind, I realize. He must sense how terrified I am.

After he finishes, he carries the paper to the desk and passes a handful of twenties for the visit and x-ray. "They'll call her back in a few minutes," the lady tells him.

He returns to the seat next to me, and I lean against him. He told the lady that I'm his girlfriend. I can play that part for an x-ray, I tell myself.

Josue smiles and wraps an arm around me. It's oddly comforting, so I don't move away when his hand settles on my waist.

We sit beside each other like a young couple in love for a few more minutes before a door at the back of the empty waiting room opens, and a young man calls my name. Well, not my name. My fake name.

Josue immediately picks me up again and carries me across the room to the doorway. We follow the man to an x-ray room, where he explains to us how he wants me to be positioned on the table.

"Is there any chance you're pregnant?" the guy asks me as I'm getting into position. A thick lead shield is being draped across my chest and lower abdomen.

I shake my head, perhaps too quickly. "We're waiting for marriage," I say.

Josue nods. "Not pregnant," he tells the guy.

"Alright," he tells us both. He asks Josue to step outside for a moment. I see the concern in his eyes and smile in his direction.

"I'll be okay," I tell him. He looks like he wants to say something, but instead, he steps outside.

"Alright, stay still," the x-ray man tells me. He takes a picture, and then has me reposition my ankle.

"Ow!" I cry out as his hand pushes my foot into position.

"Stay still," he repeats.

I do, but I'm biting hard on my lip. My ankle is burning from the sudden movement, and I feel a jolt of electricity run up my leg.

"Alright," the guy says, and he walks across the room to open the door. Josue enters quickly, assessing the room, eyeing me.

"Are you okay?" he asks, not for the first time.

"It hurts," I tell him. I'm suddenly wishing for another one of those pills that makes me sleep all day. I haven't had one for two days, and my ankle hurts terribly now.

"Wait here," he says. "I'll go get the doctor."

I stay on the x-ray table with Josue next to me, holding my hand in his. We don't have to say anything to each other while we wait. We both know what we're about to find out. It's so obvious that it's been screaming at me since I tried to stand this morning.

A middle-aged woman with dark hair wrapped around her head in a fancy braid enters the room. "Hello, Maria," the woman says. I feign a smile. "I'm Dr. Castro." She walks over and shakes my hand, then Josue's, before crossing a few more feet to the monitor displaying my x-ray.

"How did you hurt yourself?" she asks.

Show time. And I'm almost in tears from the way the technician moved my foot. "I was running, and I tripped and fell."

"How did you land?" she asks, her eyes surveying the picture while her hands maneuver the mouse. She enlarges part of the image and changes the background color. White bone shifts to a darker color, in a reversal of black and white on the screen.

"I remember twisting my foot out, and then down on the ground."

"Well, you did fracture your ankle," she tells me. "Did you land on your wrist or shoulder?"

I shrug. "No, why?"

"Sometimes, when you fall badly enough to fracture a bone, there may be other injuries," she tells me.

I try to replay the fall in my mind. "Nothing else hurts," I tell her. "I think my I caught myself on my arm, but it hasn't bothered me," I say, pointing to my forearm.

"Alright," she says. "This is a small fracture. It should heal nicely."

Josue interjects, "Will she need a cast?"

The doctor smiles. "I can give her something better. How about a walking boot?"

"Really?" I ask. "I get to walk?"

The doctor flips the picture back to regular colors, and nods. "Yes. Just follow up with your regular doctor within a week so that you can get new x-rays."

"Alright."

Josue thanks the doctor. "May I take a picture of the x-ray with my phone, to show the next doctor?" he asks. The doctor allows him to take a picture and points out the area where a tiny piece of bone from a something called a "fibula" chipped off on the side of my ankle.

I listen intently as they discuss my fracture, and then the doctor excuses herself, saying that the technician will be back to place my walking boot on my ankle.

"I'm so sorry," Josue says, wrapping his arms around me in a sudden hug. It's my fault, really, because I let him hold onto me in the waiting room. And I'm so scared of what it means to have a fractured ankle and how this will affect my chances for a scholarship, so I hug him back. It feels nice to have someone holding onto me. I've been so scared and the week that I wandered around in Mexico before I found him was terrifying. I was terrified that someone would hurt me. Or that I wouldn't find my way home. And now, in this moment, when my life just shattered even further into pieces, his arms are surprisingly comforting.

He only steps away when the technician returns with a tall black boot. It's made of something sturdy and has velcro edges. He molds it around my foot and cuts back the excess velcro. "Try to stand," he tells me.

I reach for Josue's hand and put my good foot down first, followed by my boot. A jolt of pain runs up my leg, but then, it dies down. I stand solidly on both feet, waiting for the next shock of electricity. It doesn't come.

"Wow," I say.

Josue interlaces his fingers into mine and holds onto me. Right, I'm his girlfriend. "Do you think you can walk?" he asks. When I nod, he looks a little disappointed.

"Alright, you two. Try not to break anything else," the technician teases. Josue flashes him a quick smile and we walk together towards the hallway. After the hallway, next we cross the almost empty waiting room. There's now a young mother seated with two little kids, one of which is coughing.

"Time to go home," he says, and I don't question his word choice.

TWENTY-FOUR

"How do you feel?" Josue asks when we've arrived back at his house.

"Okay," I lie. My leg feels heavy and it's tiring to carry that large boot with every step. He walks beside me, his hand holding my waist as we walk. He doesn't have to pretend anymore. Yet, here we are, and he's still holding onto me.

When we make it to the porch, he gestures towards the swing that I'd only been able to stare at a few days ago. "Do you want to sit with me?" he asks.

I can't think of a reason not to. He's been kind to me, and he listened to me about my ankle. He'd even apologized to me when he realized I'd actually broken it.

I sit down first, and he sits beside me. I shouldn't do it, but I lean against him again. There's something comforting about not being alone. I think I understand now how couples make it through long, hard marriages. It's easier to get through difficult times when someone is beside you.

It starts simply enough. His hand is on my lower back, and I'm leaning against his chest. He starts moving his hand slowly, massaging muscles that aren't even hurting. I should move away, but I don't.

The sun starts to go down behind the mountains, and we're still sitting next to each other on the bench. I'm drifting off to sleep when I feel his lips press against my forehead. Soft, warm. They send a ripple of a new tingling sensation from where he's touched me, and I'm suddenly looking up at him. What do I do?

And he answers for me. His lips move closer again, and they're on my lips, pushing against me. At first, I'm stunned, but then, I pull away. I gasp for air.

"Josue," I say once I've caught my breath. "I'm fifteen."

"I know," he says. "I shouldn't have done that."

He's watching me, and I am entranced by the twinkling in his eyes. He really likes me, and he's been kind to me. But this isn't right. "Can I call my parents?" I ask.

Like a lightning bolt has struck in between us, we both move away from each other. The easy embrace has eroded, and I'm sitting in my own corner of the wooden swing. My leg is sore, and my chest is fluttering. I don't know what to do.

I love the smell of fresh, desert air. Usually I inhale it greedily when I run. But now, I'll always associate that smell with the feel of his lips on mine. I absently touch my fingertips to my lips, wondering what it would feel like to kiss him again.

"Maybe later," he offers. "Let's get you inside."

But he doesn't have to carry me anymore, so I stand on my own two feet and begin the slow walk back into his house. His hand reaches for mine, but I flatten my hands against my hips and avoid him.

When I enter the house, I walk towards the small dining room table and take a seat. He follows my lead and sits beside me. "Are you hungry?" he asks.

"A little," I answer, realizing suddenly that I'm starving. He'd bought us some tacos on the drive back earlier in the day, but then we'd sat outside for the whole afternoon.

And I can't. I'm fifteen, and he's my freaking coyote.

He stands and goes to the kitchen. I could stand and go anywhere in the house, but now that I have my ability to walk back, I don't feel like doing anything at all. I sit and wait for him to make us something for dinner.

Darkness is beginning to fall around us, and I feel like I'm lost in another time and place. How long has it been since I've seen my parents? My little brothers? I'm trapped in a nightmare and I have no idea how I'm going to get back home.

TWENTY-FIVE

The next morning, I sit up in bed with newfound energy. Today is the day! My family finally came up with the money. Josue is going to have them drop it off somewhere, and his friend will bring it to him.

It sounds so simple. He gets paid, and I get to go home.

I can't wait to go home.

I wonder how my parents managed to come up with three thousand dollars.

I miss my brothers the most, but also my parents. I want to get back into school; I know I'm so far behind in my classes. And I won't be able to run this season, but I figure I'm already behind, so I need to get back as soon as possible.

"So, your friend will get the money?" I ask Josue when he rolls over to face me. The smile on his face fades instantly.

"I'm going to miss you," he tells me, his lips curving downward.

I nod. I've gotten used to this man in ways that I can't explain. But I don't reciprocate his response.

He waits, and I don't say anything. "Yes, my friend will pick it up. He'll call when he has it."

I haven't asked for any details about his "friend," and he hasn't disclosed any. The less I know about how he operates his business, the safer my family and I will be. I know that Josue is dangerous, even though right now, in this moment, he's looking at me with sad eyes.

He's back to brooding again. Something about the way his mood fluctuates sets off warning bells in my head, but I need this to work out so badly. I need to go home.

"Shayla," he tells me. I wait. He shakes his head and doesn't say whatever is on his mind. I don't fill in the empty space between us. Instead, I push my legs over the side of the bed and place my feet on the ground.

I stand forcefully and wobble slightly. He's already at my side as I reach backwards for the bed to steady myself. It isn't right, and I can't explain it, but he places a hand behind my back and holds me upright. I stare directly ahead, at his bare chest. The sun has barely started to rise, and even though the day is new, the desert warmth fills the space between us. I close my eyes. Holy crap, I don't know what to do.

But he does. He's older than me, wiser. He pulls me close to him and squeezes me into a hug. I try not to react to him, but it's surprisingly exciting and terrifying to be cared for by a guy.

"I need to go home," I say, just as my cheek touches against his warm skin. "My parents are so worried about me."

"I know," he says.

"When are you meeting your friend?" I want to escape his grasp, but at the same time, I'm not sure if I really do. Something is completely wrong with me, and I know my Mami would slap me if she saw me right now. I'm always so level-headed. So focused on whatever I'm aiming for.

But around Josue, I'm different. I'm not sure if that's good or bad, but it's real. I'm not the girl I was when I took a run in the mountains. I'm not even the girl I was when he found me, wandering in Tecate. Something about my time with this man has changed me.

He buries his lips in my hair. "I've never met anyone like you," he murmurs.

I let out a low laugh. "Josue, please," I whisper. "Fifteen."

He lets go a little and stares into my eyes. This is my fault. I leaned against him in clinic, I sorta maybe kissed him back a little on the swing yesterday. I held his hand and made him like me more. Something has changed between us, and it can't be reversed.

"Really, Shayla, I'm going to miss you."

I nod. "I know."

It's like I've given him permission, because suddenly he's kissing me again and I feel his arms wrapping tightly around me. I turn my head away. "Josue, please stop," I tell him. My voice is flat, devoid of emotion. I can't let him know how torn I am.

He does. He releases his arms from me and takes a step back. "I'm sorry," he says, his lower lip quivering a little.

I drop my gaze down to his chest. He has a tattoo over his heart, shaped like an eagle over a river. There are two animals sitting alongside the river; a large turtle and a smaller one. The water appears to shimmer, but really, the tattoo is only in that dark ink color that gang members use when they decorate each other.

He notices that I'm staring at his tattoo. "It's a memory," he says. He doesn't explain, and I won't ask. I'm curious, but I need to back away from this man. I've never felt this way before, and it frightens me.

Instead of talking about the electric current running between us, I look away. I've stared at his other tattoos over the past several weeks, but this one feels personal. Like he has a story to share.

Like he's meant to share a story.

"I've missed too much school." I try to say it casually, but when I glance at him, his lips are curved downward. He doesn't like this conversation. I'm not sure how to pass the next few hours until he takes me home.

He reaches for my hand to steady me. I am not even aware that I am off balance until his hand finds mine again. He starts to walk with me towards the doorway. Slow pace, careful over the small bump on the floor between his bedroom and the hallway. His hand shifts from my hand to my waist as we walk together to the dining room. He prepares to release me by the table, but I hesitate. "I can help make breakfast."

Josue's smile returns. I've decided that I like that smile. We walk in our slow-step fashion together, towards the kitchen. That funny part of me that's been gnawing at me all week makes me realize I'm actually going to miss him. Me, the girl who has never liked a boy, will miss this strange creature that is both kind and frightening, wrapped up in a broken package and marked with tattoos.

"Do you want to make pancakes?" he asks.

I smile. "Sure."

TWENTY-SIX

The day passes slowly. I'm filled with nervous anticipation. I want to see my parents and my pesky little brothers. I can't believe I'm really going home!

After Josue leaves, I'm filled with an indescribable tension. I pace around the house, looking for something. I'm not quite sure what it is; but I've packed my plastic bag of clothes and repacked it four times before I finally settle on the front porch. I hover between sitting and leaning against the little wooden enclosure around his porch. I've stared out at his fields for hours, counted every tree and made maps of the land in my mind. If my ankle wasn't broken, I could've run through the back fields, over the hills, and made my way to the mountainous highway weeks ago.

Dust kicks up on the road, and I know it's him. Nobody else has ever come here. I quickly return to my seat, feeling mutinous for all my thoughts of escape. Why would I even be considering an escape, when my coyote fee has been paid, and I'm going home?

When his car rolls around the final bend, I'm seated on the bench again. He doesn't need to see me acting so nervous. After all, I'm going home today. What I really need to be thinking about is how I'll work however many hours Mami needs me to bus tables and smile awkwardly at customers to raise money for our debt, while getting caught up on my missed schoolwork.

Josue parks his car and lingers inside for a moment before getting out. I can see him staring at me from the front seat. A chill runs down my spine. Suddenly, his eyes remind me of that crow, back in my parents' yard.

I don't know why I didn't make the comparison before. But he has always been more wild than tame.

When he stands, he looks like regular Josue. He walks the short distance from his car to the wooden swing where I'm seated. I make an extraordinary effort to remain completely still. "Hi," I say to him. "Did you get it?"

"Yes."

He sits down next to me and reaches for me. I'm confused, but I let him pull me against his side. His left arm is draped over me. I absently run my fingers across a tribal tattoo that runs along his bicep. It's a wreath of wiry thorns, and it encircles his arm, underneath an elaborate dragon.

"Are you taking me home?" I whisper.

"No."

My hand freezes over the mouth of the dragon. I've been playing with fire all week. I never should have kissed this man.

"Why not?"

"I can't lose you," he says.

I try to sit up, but his arm is suddenly strong and pins me against him. "Shayla, you're different," he tells me.

I can't see his face. For some crazy reason, I feel like if I can look him in the eyes, I will know if I'm safe or not. Honestly, I'm not sure if I'm ready to know. "My parents paid," I say. My mouth feels dry; like I'm caught in limbo in the middle of a desert, and everywhere I turn is just sand.

"Yeah," he says, sighing deeply. "They did."

"They couldn't afford it!" My voice is rising. "They barely make enough to get by, and you took their money, knowing you wouldn't give me back!" I'm angry now; pushing against him to try to sit. He tightens his grip. "Josue, you're hurting me," I tell him, twisting my neck just enough to see his face.

His eyes are dark, haunted. "Shayla," he says evenly.

I take a deep breath. "I'm fifteen," I remind him. I know he knows this.

"I'm only a few years older," he says, somewhat defensively.

"Seven years older," I counter.

"Ay, Shayla," he mutters, looking away. His grip relaxes as he stares out at his fields. All this land; purchased on the blood, sweat, and tears of migrants. At three thousand dollars a head. I shiver, wondering about the people who came here before me. Where did he keep them?

I sit up and try to move away, but his hand lingers on my shoulder. I look out at the field to see what he might be staring at. The rows of fruit trees line the back of his ranch, glistening with ripening fruit. The wild, dry grass is in need of a trim, and almost as if to drive home that point, it's wrapping around the bottom tire edges of a tractor lying in wait near the storage building in his backyard.

The building. I reach for his hand on my shoulder, hoping to ease his fingertips off my skin, but he captures them in his hand and holds on for a moment. He looks back at me. "Shayla, you're different. I've never met a girl like you." He smiles, "A young woman like you."

"I'm not a young woman. I'm still a kid," I tell him.

But he doesn't agree, and he doesn't let me go. He pulls me into that familiar yet uncomfortable space next to him and keeps an arm draped around my shoulder, while he stares out at his land and I glance from him to the building in the back.

The sun moves in the sky, downward, and brilliant hues of pink and purple are painted above us. Night falls, and we're still seated together. Not talking, not figuring out where we go from here.

When he finally turns to check on me, it's then that he notices the steady stream of tears down my cheeks. "Shayla," he says again. "We could be something, you and me. I care about you." He reaches his free hand to wipe away my tears, but that triggers a flood.

I shake my head. "Josue, if you care about me, then take me home."

He shrugs. "You'll get used to me," he says.

I bite my lip, feeling the warm, metallic taste of a new wound between my teeth. "No. I won't."

He sighs heavily. "Shayla, let's go inside."

My head moves from side to side in disagreement. "No."

"Where do you expect to sleep?" he asks, chuckling. I must be a stupid little girl to him. I'm angry, scared, and desperately homesick. I lift my arm and point to the building in the back. "Shayla," he says, but I don't answer him. "Fine. You'll change your mind," he declares. Then he stands and guides me across the field to the building I've been wondering about for the past few weeks.

***

"I'll come check on you later," he tells me.

I shrug and pretend to ignore him. The truth is, he's impossible to ignore. He's tall, strong, moody, and a weird mixture of frightening and sometimes caring. I haven't figured out what to do. I wait for him to leave, prepared to try to walk off this property and back to the main road. But I hear the sound of a key turning sharply in the lock.

Of course, the door locks from the outside. I count to one hundred four times before walking to the doorway and testing the knob. It doesn't open. I pull again, but nothing happens.

I'm trapped.

It's then that I decide to survey my surroundings. It's dark, so I can't see where the light switches are located. I put my hand in front of me and walk slowly across the room, trying to get my bearings. Apparently, I'm in a large, open space.

My foot makes contact with a hard surface. I pause and bend downward to figure out what is in front of me. Scratchy linen over a mattress. My hands measure the space in front of me and I carefully turn and sit. I've found a bed.

The mattress is too thin, and the springs creak under my weight. It feels old, worn. Many people have crossed through this place.

Many people, at three thousand dollars apiece.

I wonder what my parents had to do to come up with the money. And I worry about how they must feel now that they've paid and I'm not being returned to them.

Brenden and Esteban are probably sitting on our old living room sofa, staring at the telephone. I imagine that they're all waiting for news of where to meet me and my coyote.

My coyote.

How could I have been so stupid?

I suck in a deep breath and try to fight the rise of emotions that is coursing through me. My heart is racing so fast that I can't keep track of how fast it's beating. My eyes burn with unshed tears. I lay down in the bed and succumb to the moment. "I want to go home," I say out loud. My throat smolders with rising bile.

"I want to go home!" I shout. Tears stream down my cheeks and I fight back the urge to retch. A series of garbled cries follows as I beat my fist into the mattress.

If Josue comes back, I'll stand up to him. I'll demand that he sends me home. It's been too long, and I miss my family. He has no right to keep me. No right at all.

The air around me is thick and cool, and the night progresses with no sign of Josue. Long after the crying subsides and my breathing has returned to a slow, even pace, I realize that he's not coming for me. I close my eyes and begin to count, hoping for sleep. Hoping for a chance to go home. Hoping for anything but this; I have no idea what Josue is planning and I'm suddenly terrified.

TWENTY-SEVEN

Morning comes, and Josue has not returned. Daylight creeps through a crack under the door, giving a strange eerie glow to the room. I squint my eyes until I can make out a light switch on the far wall, close to the entrance.

I stand up too quickly, feeling a small jolt of pain in my ankle. "Oops," I mutter as I cross the room slowly. I don't want to bump into anything with my booted foot.

When I reach the wall and flip the switch, nothing happens. The light doesn't turn on. I feel all the resolve in my body slipping away. I can't do this. I can't stay trapped in a dark building.

I take a few small steps and reach the door. The light from underneath tells me that he must be awake. I ball up my fist and slam it into the door, hard. Again. Again. I start beating on the door and screaming at the top of my lungs.

"Josue!" I yell. "Let me out!"

The door doesn't budge. There's no sound from outside; no opening of a door or the heavy sound of his feet on dirt. I pound on the door until my hand is sore, and then I pound harder. My throat is scratchy from yelling his name. And my bladder is full.

I turn back to the dark room behind me. I don't know where the bathroom is, and I really don't want to walk around in the dark. My ankle is already broken from our mountainous trek across the border.

A clanging sound catches my attention, and I twirl back to face the door. "Josue!" I yell again.

The noise approaches; keys on a keyring. He's coming for me.

He locked me in here.

I swallow hard and wait for the door to open. The key turns slowly in the lock, and the door opens outward. He's standing in front of me, a strange look on his face.

"What did you do to your hand?" he asks me.

Everything is suddenly bright and visible. I glance down at my hand and notice the ugly purple bruise that's formed on the side of my right hand, below my pinky fingers. There's a fresh cut over the last two knuckles, and blood is oozing out.

"You locked me in here," I whisper, and then start crying. I bite my lip, trying to make the tears stop, but they won't. I'm trembling when he tries to wrap his arms around me, and I push back against him. "It's cold and dark and I have to pee," I tell him. I stretch out my hands and hold them against his chest, pushing him away. "Don't touch me."

"Shayla, you told me to put you in here," he says. His arms fall to his sides, motionless. The dragon's face collapses away, out of sight as his arm shifts away.

I shake my head. "No. Not like this."

"Shayla, please," he says. "You're bleeding, let's go back to the house so you can get cleaned up."

His eyes seem softer, concerned. He is watching me, waiting for me to give in.

"Can I have a flashlight?" I ask. "You can't leave me in the dark."

His chest rises and falls under my hands. I can feel his heartbeat underneath the palm of my hand, and I know I just keep making mistakes with this man. "Shayla, please," he says quietly. His voice is soft, like when Papi is standing next to Mami in the kitchen and they're talking about how their days have been or reminiscing about their previous life in Guatemala.

"Josue, I want to go home." I realize that I'm still holding onto him and pull my hands away. The sudden loss of contact feels like a circuit has been disconnected.

"I'm not ready to let you go," he says.

"My parents paid you," I remind him, folding my arms over my chest. I notice a trace of blood on his shirt where my hand had been.

He sighs. "You're right. I shouldn't have taken their money," he tells me.

I gasp. "Yes, you should have. It's payment for bringing me home," I say. "So please, bring me home."

He shakes his head firmly, his eyes staring at me more intently now. He glances from me to the dark room behind me, then back to me again. "Shayla, are you coming into the house with me, or staying here? We can make breakfast again," he offers. His lips are on alert; ready to shift into a smile or a frown, depending on my answer. I have no idea why I have such a strong effect on him, but I don't want to be near him.

I bite my lower lip again, drawing blood. I feel a slow trickle under my teeth and shake my head slowly. "I'm not hungry," I say, but my stomach gurgles its dissent. My eyes dart to the dragon on his arm. It has a row of thick scales on its back. I need to be strong like a dragon, I tell myself.

"Shayla," he says my name again. He reaches for me, and his thumb traces my lower lip. I take another deep breath and look back up at him. He withdraws his hand, and I see red smeared on his fingertip.

For whatever it's worth, Josue doesn't seem like he wants to hurt me. I'm not sure why he kept me or what he's trying to prove to me, but at the moment, I realize that none of those things matter. I really need to go to the bathroom, and whether I want to admit it or not, I'm actually hungry. My stomach growls at that moment, just to prove that point to me. "I want to stay mad at you," I tell him.

"Fine. But at least come inside with me."

I'm tired and my back hurts from the box springs in the mattress. I don't want to cave in, but I find my head nodding involuntarily. "Okay," I finally whisper.

TWENTY-EIGHT

"I envy you," Josue says to me after breakfast. He made breakfast burritos that we both ate in silence. We're sitting on the sofa in his living room, and my eyes feel heavy from bad sleep and a full belly.

I look over at him. He's on the next cushion, leaning towards me a little. "Why?"

He frowns. "I wonder what it would be like to have parents and siblings. A family."

His eyes look sad. I don't know why that bothers me, but it does. "What do you mean?" I ask. As I say it, I realize how little I know about him. I've collected small fragments of his life story over the past few weeks, but he doesn't offer too many details.

Almost everything I've learned about him has been a small puzzle piece from an infinity sized puzzle. I have no idea why he's like this, or how I can convince him to set me free.

"I'm completely alone," he says. He turns away from me, staring across the room instead. I look to see what he's looking at. There's a small photo frame on the large entertainment center across from us. Above the flat screen tv that we haven't turned on. It's the only photo I've seen in the whole house. I don't know how I didn't see it sooner, and now that I see it, I want to look more closely. "I have this giant piece of land, and no one to share it with."

His words scare me. I keep my eyes focused on the photograph. "Who's that?" I ask, my voice cautious.

Josue stands and crosses the room to bring the picture to me. He hands the wooden frame to me; it's a grainy black and white picture of a young woman and a little boy. The woman has a serious expression on her face, and her hair is long and wavy. Her cheekbones are high, and her eyes remind me of Josue. She's wearing a flowery blouse and a long, flowing skirt. I imagine that there is a mix of vibrant colors in the patterns on her skirt, but they're hidden away in greyscale. The little boy is small, perhaps three or four years old. He has dark hair and a goofy expression on his face. He looks thin but healthy.

"My mother," he says.

Before I can stop myself, I say, "Tell me about her."

He leans closer to me, but it almost feels like he's trying to get closer to the picture instead of trying to invade my space. He has a haunted look in his eyes as he speaks. "She loved me so much. And I didn't realize it," he says. He takes the picture back from me. "She was deported when I was a kid, and she died trying to get back to me."

Josue's words hang in the air between us. I watch as he stands and puts the picture away. He doesn't sit back down. "How old were you?" I ask.

He's pacing. His long legs make an easy stride across the room as he makes his way over to the window. He stares into the backyard, his eyes lost somewhere in the fruit grove. "Five."

"She was beautiful," I say.

He nods but doesn't look back at me. He continues to stare out the window for a long time, and I lean my head against the cushion on the sofa. I'm emotionally spent, and I don't know what to say to him. Or if I should even say anything at all.

I close my eyes and allow myself to drift away. As I fade into sleep, I dream of a small turtle and its mama, sitting beside a lazy river.

***

When I awaken, I'm sprawled out over the sofa at an uncomfortable angle. My foot feels sore in the large boot. I look around, but Josue isn't in the room with me.

I sit up and listen closely for the telltale sound of his presence.

Nothing.

I stand up, the achy feeling in my ankle growing stronger. I walk to the hallway and glance in both directions. Should I go to the kitchen and check outside? Or to the bedroom?

My ankle decides for me. The pain is almost unbearable, so I start down the hallway towards Josue's bedroom.

When I enter the room, I expect to see him. But I don't. I'd rather not try to figure out where he is, I realize. I have one goal.

I go to his dresser and open the drawer that he's set aside for me. He's done laundry again, and my clothes are neatly folded in rows. I pick a shirt, shorts, and clean underwear before heading to the bathroom.

I've been wanting to soak my foot for days. The bathtub is impressively large. I place the stopper over the drain and turn on the water. He doesn't have any bubble bath, so I pour two capfuls of shampoo into the water and watch the foamy bubbles begin to form. When the layer of bubbles is artfully tall and the water looks just right, I turn off the faucet and begin the task of removing the velcro straps on my walking boot.

The last time I looked at my foot was in the urgent care clinic. When I remove the boot, it's apparent that the purplish bruise has started to fade into a golden-brown color. My ankle is still swollen and there's a small blister forming.

I undress and lower myself into the bathtub, grateful for a moment of peace.

At home, there's no privacy. We share one bathroom and the bathtub is tiny. Here, I'm practically floating in the giant oval tub. I feel guilty for liking this man's house, but it's really nice to stay in a place that isn't so tiny.

And is so secluded. I cringe.

I soak in the water, letting my ankle relax. When the bubbles fade away, I add more soap and more water, until a new layer rises up. It's then that I hear a knock on the door.

"Hey, are you okay in there?" Josue's strong voice calls through the wooden door frame.

I smooth out a layer of bubbles over my skin and sigh. "I'm fine," I say.

He takes the hint and doesn't knock again. I stay in the bathroom until all my fingers and toes are wrinkled and my foot feels a little better. I stand up, trying not to place too much weight on my ankle. It's sore, but I don't feel the electric jolt of pain this time. I quickly get dressed and gather my dirty clothes and boot into my hand. I want to put a band aid over the blister before I put the boot back on.

"Are you still okay?" Josue asks through the door.

My hands are full and I'm struggling to take a few steps. "Actually, can you help me?" I ask.

The door opens and Josue walks in. He flashes me his best smile. "How's your ankle?" he asks. He must see the blister, because his face suddenly looks concerned again.

"It hurts a little, but the water helped," I say.

"Do you want me to carry you to the bed?" he offers.

The achy feeling is returning the longer that I stand on it. "Yeah," I say softly. "I need to cover the blister before I put the boot on."

He nods and I see the edges of a smile forming as he scoops me up and carries me back to his bed. The familiar feeling of being wrapped in his arms returns, and I'm not sure if I like him or hate him. I definitely feel something for him, but I can't figure out the emotion.

He lays me down on my side of the bed.

Oh, my God. I have a side of the bed. His bed.

And then he excuses himself to fetch a band aid for me. I watch nervously as he affixes the band aid over the blister. I am so worried that it will hurt, but it's practically painless. "Perfect," he tells me. He rests his hand on my lower leg, just above my ankle. It shouldn't, but it sends a tingly sensation up my leg.

"Thank you," I say. He nods, that boyish grin on his face growing.

He releases his hand and shoves his hands into his pockets. I definitely notice the absence of his touch.

"Are you ready for dinner?" he asks.

"My leg is sore," I confide.

"No problem," he tells me. "Dinner in bed." And with that, he exits to go get whatever meal he's prepared for us.

TWENTY-NINE

My head is so mixed up. I've set up a wall of pillows between us again, and we both fell asleep. But when I wake up, I find that I've somehow crossed the barrier, and I'm lying beside him, my arm across his chest. I'm not sure why I keep letting myself get close to him.

No wonder we're both so confused.

I start to move my arm, but he stirs in his sleep and pulls me into a tighter embrace. It feels nice to not be alone. But it's also terrifying.

His hand comes to life and begins moving slowly on my upper back. Small, perfect circles. I cave in and rest my head on his chest. It feels oddly nice to be held by a man.

I calculate that I'm almost sixteen and want to slap myself for having that thought. I am too young to date, and this man is not an option. I want to slip away from him and go back to my side of the bed, but his hand is so soothing. I lean closer instead and let out a fake snoring noise.

My ability to reason has been completely compromised. I can feel his heartbeat again, but this time with my cheek instead of my hand. It feels warm and solid against my skin. I suck in a deep breath and try to memorize every sensation, because somehow, I will get out of this house and get home soon. I just have to.

"Good night, Shayla," Josue whispers, his lips brushing against my forehead.

"Good night," I murmur back, shocked that I hadn't realized that he is also awake.

I have really lost it. Even my Papi would yell at me for this. But I nestle in against his chest and breathe in his scent, grateful that I'm not out in that dark, cool room anymore.

His fingers slow until he eventually falls asleep. I listen to the sound of his heartbeat until it lulls me into sleep, too.

***

"*Buenos dias, dormilona*," Josue whispers when I open my eyes the next morning. I'm still curled up against him on his side of the bed.

My Papi sometimes calls me *dormilona*, or at least, when Mami can't hear him. I am a bit of a sleepyhead in the mornings, so it's endearing. My Papi has a lot of cute nicknames for me. I miss his voice.

"No," I say suddenly, sitting upright. I feel like I'm gasping for air. Like I'm boxed into the little cell at the detention center. Or the cold, dark building that Josue uses to keep his travelers. I slide several inches away, back to my half of the bed.

"What happened?" Josue is asking from somewhere beside me. I suck in another deep breath, but it makes me feel more panicky.

"Josue, I want to go home," I say. I pull my knees tight against my chest and wrap my arms around my legs. The boot feels bulky over my leg, and the velcro straps scratch against my arm.

Josue is silent beside me. There isn't really anything he could say to make me feel better. Well, except for "I'll take you home."

But he doesn't.

I force myself to take several long, slow breaths. It feels like when I'm pumped for a race and I'm trying to get myself psyched up for the challenge. My heart still feels like it's speeding down a two-lane highway, winding through the mountains. But my breathing slows, and I feel like I have enough air.

He inches closer to me, draping his arm over my shoulder. I don't push him away this time. Instead, I stare at a random spot on the wall and try to focus on controlling my breathing.

"Shayla, do you think maybe we met for a reason?" he asks. His voice sounds far away.

I inhale deeply. Everything in my life made sense until I ran on the wrong trail. I had everything figured out; I had planned the perfect future for myself. But over the past month, all my plans had fallen into pieces, and this man sitting beside me had offered me so much hope. He had promised to bring me home.

"Josue, I'm a kid. This can't work," I say.

He leans closer still; his head rests so close to my own that I feel like the hair on our heads is touching. "But Shayla," he says softly. "Do you want it to work?"

I stare at my fingernails. They've gotten too long, and I really need to trim them. I try to think of anything that could distract me from what Josue is asking me.

"Shayla," Josue says softly. "Say something."

His arm feels so strong against my back. Sometimes, when he holds me, I can't tell where he ends, and I begin. I don't like that heavy feeling. Life was easier before Josue invaded my personal space and made me feel things I don't understand.

I let go of my death grip on my knees, and lift my head slightly, so that I can see his face. He looks so sad. How can this man have such a wide range of emotions? I've only known my Papi's steady demeanor, and the rowdy behavior of teen boys on my cross-country team. I've never known someone as complex as him.

His eyes are glistening, almost like he's trying not to cry. I think that's what breaks me. I'll probably dissect this moment for the rest of my life, but for now, in this moment, I lean closer to him and brush my lips against his. They're warm, soft, ready.

He kisses me back. Strong, sturdy, slow. He's wrapping his arms around me, and I let him. I miss my family, and he's keeping me from them, but I can't deny that there's some strange attraction between us. I feel reckless and lightheaded in his arms, and I'm afraid that I won't know how to stop kissing him.

Josue is the one who pulls away first. My lips burn with awareness of his closeness. He runs his fingers through my hair and down my back. I don't mean to, but I lean closer to him and dare him to kiss me again.

He looks like he really wants to, but instead, he leans back against the headboard and sighs. His arms are still around me, but he's loosened his grip.

I lay my head on his chest, over the strange river with the eagle, and listen to his heart. It's racing, just like mine. "Josue," I say, but I don't really know what I want to tell him.

"In a perfect world, we'd be together forever," he says as he places one of his hands on my cheek. I tip my face slightly, just enough to kiss the palm of his hand.

I need to go home. I'm not sure why I keep falling back into Josue's snares, but I do. He traces my lips with his thumb and watches me closely. Expectantly. Our eyes lock and everything else seems suddenly far away. I feel his hand move down my back, and I understand what he's asking for. It's not really mine to give, nor his to take. I'm too young.

"It's not a perfect world," I finally say.

He doesn't say anything. I cling to my pillow and eventually close my eyes. I can feel him still staring at me even as I drift off to sleep.

THIRTY

"Can I go home today?" I ask the following morning. I've decided to try the annoying-little-brother approach. Brenden and Esteban have trained me well.

"Not today."

"Why not?"

Josue is standing at the stove, preparing breakfast. I walk carefully past him and go sit on the porch instead.

I'm not sure what I'm hoping he'll do. He's obviously not going to take me home until he wants to. But I don't want to be complacent; I have to do something. He has to know that it isn't okay to just keep me like this.

Several minutes pass before Josue comes to the doorway. He still hasn't put on a shirt, and I find my eyes wandering over the landscape of tattoos that cover his chest. One that I haven't paid attention to before catches my eye this time; there's an outline of a river on the edge of his right chest, with something inscribed under it in Spanish.

Nunca te olvidaré.

He sees where my eyes are focused and folds his arms over his chest, covering the tattoo from my sight.

"Are you planning to eat?"

I shrug. Would that work? If I went on a hunger strike, would he release me?

My stomach growls defiantly.

"Shayla," he says, his voice suddenly soft. Kind. I shake my head, not ready to cave in just yet.

"I want to talk to them. You have to let me tell them I'm okay."

He stares at me, then sighs. "It's better this way. You'll get used to me."

I don't even know what that means. I'm pretty sure I don't want to know. I look away, my eyes watching the still land behind us. There is no wind today, and the trees are silent. There are no birds flittering around, and no cars approaching on the road.

We're in the middle of nowhere.

My ankle is broken. I don't have a phone or internet access. There's a television, but that won't help me at all.

I'm trapped.

I should keep my strength up. I glance up at him, and I'm pretty sure his eyes hold the same nervousness as mine. The ground beneath us keeps shifting, and neither of us know where we stand.

But he holds all the power.

"Shayla," he repeats. He's walking slowly towards me, and before I can even consider my next action, he's seated beside me. "You know you feel it too."

Is it awful that I do? That I feel something for this man? I don't know what to do because I can't even hide the mixed-up way that I shouldn't be feeling about him.

I lean my head against his shoulder and think through my options. I could argue with him and go back to the dark, scary backhouse. No, I won't do that. I could continue the annoying-little-brother approach, but that's what got me angry and led me to sitting on the porch without food in my belly. Or, I could give in. But maybe I don't really have to give in. Maybe I could just let him think I'm okay with this?

Because I can't be okay with this. Mami's beautiful face leaps into my memories, and I know that I have to do whatever it takes to find my way home to her.

"What do you want from me?" I ask. He shifts towards me, then wraps his arm around me. It doesn't feel as constricting as the other day, but it does feel possessive. Like he doesn't plan to ever let me go.

"You could be happy with me," Josue whispers.

His words linger between us. I don't know what to say. How could I be happy like this? I'm fifteen.

All I've ever considered is a life that helps my family.

But that other part of me thinks about the way things are everywhere else. Girls my age get married in Mexico. In Guatemala. In other countries, too. Girls don't always get to choose what's best for them. Sometimes, they choose what's best for their families. And other times, they don't have any say at all.

Is that what he's asking of me?

I close my eyes and try to think about what I want.

Because I have never really considered what I want. My dreams have always been about "we." My parents, my brothers, and me.

My dreams have never been just about me.

Do I even like to run?

I did. I used to enjoy the feeling of the wind blowing through my hair as I raced up the mountain. But now, whenever I think about running, I remember two things: the feel of the Border Patrol officer's boot against my skin, and the way Josue grabbed me before that box truck could've hit me.

No. I don't feel the same way about anything anymore.

I hated working at Mami's restaurant. Her boss always made me uncomfortable. He cheated her with my pay, and neither of us could say a word because Mami is undocumented. Even though I've always had papers, some things remain true. I'm less of a citizen because my parents aren't citizens. I've never had the same rights as everyone else.

Josue's fingers are tracing the skin on my arm. This should set me on edge, but instead, he's putting me at ease. I don't understand.

This isn't right.

I turn my face just enough to look at him. His eyes are glossy, like he's trying not to cry.

That can't be right.

"What are you thinking about?" Josue asks.

I don't answer. I pull away slowly, carefully. I don't want to upset him, and he's as skittish as me. "I don't know," I say. It's all a jumble of thoughts, anyway.

When I'm almost free from his touch, I pause and stare into his eyes. Why does he have that ability to tear at my soul, yet terrify me, too? "Do you want to know what I'm thinking?" he asks. His voice is laden with some heavy secret that he is considering telling me.

No. I really don't want to know. Nothing terrifies me more than everything about him. I shake my head slowly, not sure how to keep it light between us. My stomach growls again, giving me an out. "You're thinking that we should eat?"

He shrugs. "If you say so, Shayla."

THIRTY-ONE

How do I keep him close, yet at a distance? The lessons that I needed to protect me from Josue were never taught to me back home. Now, it's just the two of us, with no one else around for miles. We went through the motions of breakfast and lunch, and by late afternoon, I feel like I'm going mad.

"How's your ankle?" Josue asks when he approaches me on the porch. I'm leaning against the porch railing, off-loading all my weight onto my good ankle. The broken one is held slightly off the ground, just behind my stronger leg.

I consider his question. Sure, my ankle hurts, but it's healing in the walking boot. What he really wants to know is whether I'm strong enough to escape.

The sun is starting to lower itself behind the mountains, and the sky is a brilliant pink. I stare at the orchard for another long moment before I answer. Nothing needs to be fast out here.

"It hurts."

"Oh."

I turn to face him. Again, his eyes betray his thoughts. Josue is just as affected by me as I am by him. Everything really comes down to two choices.

Give in, or pretend to give in.

I'm not sure which one I'm doing as I lean towards him. He greedily takes me into his arms and pulls me close.

"Ow," I whisper, as I step sideways to adjust to his embrace.

He instantly knows that I've put too much weight on my ankle, and he lifts me up like a small child again. The same as on the mountain; he can effortlessly carry me around.

Every time I try to convince myself that I'm strong enough to escape from him, he reminds me that he's more than I've realized. I lean my head against his chest and wait for him to say something.

But he doesn't.

Instead, he silently carries me to the bench and sets me down. He sits down next to me, just close enough that out hips are touching.

I can't help it; my hands are shaking. I've never been a good actress. And the worst part is that I might not be acting.

Josue waits. That must be something he's really good at. I wonder what his life must normally be like; he brings people to their families and collects his fee, but when they're locked away in his holding cell, he's alone.

When he's waiting in Tecate, he's alone.

Everything about him is the same. He lives alone in two places. He drives alone, works alone. I've never seen him talk to anyone. No friends visit.

His mom died. He's an only child. He has no idea who is dad is.

Of course, he can wait. He knows how to sit in silence.

Surprisingly, so do I. How much of my life has been spent absorbing other people's emotions? Other people's needs?

Was that what drew me to running? I was able to escape everyone and everything, and just focus on my strength and my needs?

Josue reaches out his hand and places it on top of mine to still them. I can still feel my hand trembling slightly underneath his larger hand, but I don't want to think about it.

"I'm sorry," I mutter.

"Are you afraid of me?" Josue asks.

I don't look at him. "No."

"Are you lying?" He sounds wounded, like I've sucker-punched him.

I shrug, then confess, "I'm afraid of me."

His fingers begin to move slowly over the top of my hand, massaging the thin muscles that line my fingers. I feel his body shifting next to mine, but I don't move. I'm not sure what this thing is between us, but I think I need it to continue. Either because I want it to, or because I've decided that if it continues, he might let me go. Or he might get sloppy and I might get away.

"Can I kiss you?"

He's been kind to me, most of the time. I'm not locked in the building behind his house. He didn't leave me stranded in Tecate. He hasn't actually hurt me.

I nod slowly, still not looking at him.

He lifts his hand to my cheek, ready to tilt my face towards his.

But immediately pulls his fingers away.

"Why are you crying?"

I shrug. "I didn't realize I was."

"I haven't hurt you."

"I know." I bow my head lower. My hair is messy and frames my face before winding around my shoulders and down my back. It feels like it needs to be tightened into a braid, but I don't think my hands could handle the movement right now. Instead, I swipe away the tears and wait.

His arm settles around my shoulder and I slide back into a comfortable position. It's easy to relax against him when I don't think about what he's done. When I don't remember that he's keeping me from my family.

"You told me that your dream is to get a scholarship, so you can help your family," Josue says, his voice cracking slightly as he speaks. "What if you could bypass all of that hardship and have everything you need, now?"

"What do you mean?" This time, I actually turn my head in his direction and meet his eyes.

He smiles. His face always looks so much more peaceful when he lets himself smile; I realize. "What if this is what you need? You could stay here with me, and I could take care of you."

"How does that help my family?"

"I have enough land for all of you."

It's tempting. Everything I've ever wanted, easier. Without the sacrifice. Only, it is a sacrifice. All I have to do is agree to stay with a dangerous man, a coyote. I won't ask, but I'm certain that he's done very bad things before. He's too quick, too smart. His eyes see more than mine do, and I study everything.

"I…" I look out at his fields again, but it's darker now. Shadows have fallen over everything that he's offering me. "Can I think about it?"

There must be clouds in the sky tonight, because even the stars are hidden. I let out a breath that I've been holding for too long and tuck a long strand of hair behind my ear before nuzzling my head back against his chest.

I hate how it feels like I belong here.

How can a person want two different things?

THIRTY-TWO

Every morning feels the same. I wake up next to Josue, and then one of us gets up first. He always seems to be awake, even when his eyes are closed.

Nine days have passed since he didn't give me back to my parents. In those nine days, I've gone through a tidal wave of emotions. I've been angry, sad, scared, nervous, and sometimes, I've had bursts of happiness.

"Hey," Josue says, staring at me.

His dark eyes hold so many mysteries.

I remember the night before he was supposed to take me home, and the way he held me all night. We haven't been that close since then, but I'm trying to build myself up to letting him trust me. Even though I don't trust him at all.

"Hi."

"Come here," he says, lifting the sheet up so that I can lay down against his bare skin. He never wears a shirt to bed, and I wonder if I've made him change his habits because he does wear shorts or sweatpants. He doesn't seem to own pajama pants, though.

I obediently tread the space between us and lay down beside him. My head rests against his chest, right over the lake with the two turtles. I've since figured out that they represent him and his mom.

He doesn't ask for more than hugs or kisses, which makes me feel incredibly relieved. I'm not ready to take this any further. I keep remembering that I'm only fifteen, even if he doesn't.

I listen to his heartbeat for a long time, not daring to move away. Josue has been surprisingly clingy over the past week. I trace the words on the right side of his chest, next to the river. "What does this mean?" I ask, referring to the words in Spanish.

Nunca te olvidaré.

"I'll never forget you."

His mom. I think about that photo in his living room; the only trace he has left of her.

I decide in that moment that he won't hurt me. He's terrifying and probably has a past that would shame me in front of my parents. But he's my only way home, and I haven't come up with any other plans.

I press my lips against his chest in a soft kiss, and then trace a small row of kisses up to his cheek. He's lying completely still, waiting. Watching me. His lips are parted just a little, like he wants to say something.

"Are we boyfriend and girlfriend?" I ask innocently, when my lips are next to his.

"Is that what you want?"

I nod slowly. "I think so," I tell him softly. Instinctively, I know which words to use with him. I've gotten to know him better than I'd realized.

"Then yes."

I smile, then place my lips on his. We kiss for a long time, until I finally free myself from his lips because I'm in an awkward position. "I need to get up," I tell him as I scooch away. I rub my ankle for emphasis. He hops out of bed and grabs my boot.

If I was a fairytale princess, it might be cute that he knows how to put my boot on. After all, their stories were somewhat archaic, like mine. I shrug the thought aside. It's been nine days since my parents paid their fee, and I have to do whatever it takes to get home.

Even if I feel incredibly conflicted about everything.

***

"What do you want to do today?" Josue asks over coffee and huevos rancheros. It's a Mexican dish with fried tortillas, veggies, salsa, and sunny side up eggs. I'm realizing that I mostly know Guatemalan dishes, even though I've spent my whole life within walking distance of Mexico.

Well, within running distance.

"I don't know. I'm feeling kinda stir-crazy."

"Hmm?"

"I mean, I only left the ranch to go to the doctor, and that was weeks ago. I was hoping…" I let my voice trail off, then shake my head. "Never mind, it was a silly idea."

Josue has that intense look in his eyes, the one that he gets when he's worrying about something. It doesn't hurt that I kissed him awake and became his official girlfriend, maybe, but I need to tread lightly.

Because I finally came up with a plan.

"What were you thinking?" he asks. His voice sounds too wary, too uncomfortable.

"Nothing, babe," I say, adding a term of endearment. "Maybe we can pick some pomegranates later?"

I've always loved to eat them, but they're incredibly expensive. I can't believe he has a whole orchard with thirty-two trees. I've counted them and recounted them. He's sitting on a gold mine.

Bought by coyote fees.

I plaster a smile on my face to hide my frustration.

He hasn't said anything yet. He's looking at me weirdly.

"And maybe some oranges? But not too many. I don't want to waste anything."

"Babe?" he finally repeats.

I shrug. "I thought I'd try it out. It didn't fit. I'll find the right word." Like coyote. Keeper of citizen-migrant girl. Boyfriend. My smile starts to waver; I can feel the edges of my lips curving downward.

"It's okay," he says, chuckling. "I think I like it. But only if I can say it, too?"

"Mmm-hmm," I say, taking another bite of eggs. If my mouth is full, I can't say something stupid.

"Alright, babe." He winks at me, and I force another smile.

THIRTY-THREE

Picking fruit proves to be challenging. I can't reach anything, and even if I could reach it by standing on my tippy-toes, I can't because I've got my bulky walking boot.

Josue lifts me up onto his shoulders and asks me to pick the fruit from high above the ground. If we were really dating, it might be cute. But I feel dizzy, swaying behind his head.

His hands hold firmly to my free leg and my boot. I've got one of those reusable shopping bags looped over my shoulder and I quickly pick a handful of pomegranates and drop them into the bag. I don't like being up so high.

But it does give me a vantage point I hadn't considered. I can see just a little more of his land, and I see that there's a thicker forest just over the hill beyond the orchard.

If I'm still stuck here after my ankle heals, maybe that's where I'll go. I imagine an escape plan, but he's already lifting me down from his shoulders and placing me back on solid ground before I can imagine it completely.

"Are you okay?"

"Hmm?" I ask.

"Your cheeks are flushed. You were really quiet."

I sigh. "I felt dizzy. I didn't like being up so high."

He nods. "We won't do that again, then," he tells me. "Do you feel like walking?"

Josue takes the bag from me and places it on his other shoulder, away from me. His hand automatically loops into mine, and when our fingers are intertwined, I exhale. I would be lying if I pretended that nothing was happening between us. I never understood what a love-hate relationship was until I met him.

But I don't love him. I just like him. Too much.

"Okay."

We walk slowly from tree to tree, and he tells me the story of each one. "This was my first tree," he says, touching the bark of a lime tree. "I bought a small sapling at the flea market, and I planted it here. I wanted to see if I could make something grow."

I reach out my hand and touch the smooth bark. "You did."

"Shayla, I came from nothing. I had nothing. And I always thought this would be enough."

I don't want him to profess how he feels about me, so I do what feels natural. I lean against his chest and breathe in his scent. I'm not sure when I started to recognize an odor that was distinctly Josue, but I know him in ways I've never known anyone.

"I'm glad you want to be my girlfriend."

My fingertips linger on the tree trunk, and I nod slowly. Right. Girlfriend. "It feels strange," I say, testing the air with my words. "I always thought boyfriends and girlfriends go out on dates."

I'm not looking at him, but I hear Josue let out a sigh. He moves in closer to where I'm standing, his hand automatically settling over my lower back.

"Is that what you want, Shayla? You want to go out on a date?"

I shrug. Somehow, I know that I need to play it cool. "It might be fun. I mean, if you want to."

He brushes his lips against my forehead, and I wait for him to say something. A long moment passes between us. I wonder what he must be thinking. But I won't speak the words that are probably rattling through his head.

"You're right. We could go out for dinner."

I tilt my head towards him and smile as happily as I can. "Really?"

This can work. I don't have a plan, but somehow, I'll make sure my parents can find me. Somehow.

"Anything for you, Shayla," he tells me. I know that isn't quite true. Anything for me that keeps me here. I feel chained, but for the first time since he didn't return me to my parents, I can imagine finding my way home to them.

My throat feels dry and I can't trust my voice, so I lean against him and let him hug me again. It's better to say less, anyway.

COYOTE (Human Smuggler)

THIRTY-FOUR

Last year, I went through a phase where I tried to learn all the fancy long-haired braids. I've always kept my hair long and braided it in either one or two standard braids, but everyone was doing cool new styles and I wanted to learn.

I'm standing in front of the bathroom mirror, working my hair into two elaborate fishtail braids. The one on the left is perfect, but I undo the one on the right for the third time and start over.

Josue passes by the doorway to check on me. I've purposely left the door open so that he can see me making a fuss over getting ready. I don't want him to suspect anything, so I have to be careful.

"Wow, Shayla," I hear him say from behind me. I glance back in the mirror at his reflection and smile.

"Do you like it?"

Josue nods, his eyes locked with mine in the mirror. It feels nice to have him compliment me, even though our overall situation is awful. I want to go home, and he doesn't want to let me go. We can't continue wanting opposite things without expecting one of us to get hurt.

"You're blushing."

I look back at my face and laugh quietly. "Go away, Josue. You're making me nervous."

He nods and goes back to whatever he's been doing all day. He's spent most of the day staring at something on his phone, and he left briefly for an hour after lunch. When he came back, he gave me a brand-new dress with spaghetti straps.

Sometimes he's too good with sizing and style. It makes me wonder more about his Coyote business, but then, I don't think I really want to know why he knows my size or what would look nice on me. Instead, I admire my reflection after I correct the braid for the final time.

The dress is navy blue with tiny white flowers, and it reaches just above my knees. My boot is awkwardly tall, but I'm guessing he didn't want to get a long dress for me because maybe I might trip. Or, because it's barely the beginning of fall in the desert, so maybe he couldn't find one.

When I walk out of the bathroom, Josue slips his phone into his pocket and stands up immediately. "You look great," he tells me.

"Thank you."

"Seriously, Shayla, you look amazing."

I can feel my cheeks growing warmer. I never wear makeup, but at this rate, I won't have to. My cheeks are going to be permanently pink from his comments.

"I feel like a princess," I tell him, drawing another smile from him. He's smiled more for me today then over the past few weeks, although every time he looks at his phone, his eyes gloss over and he looks worried.

"You are a princess."

I wait for him to make the next move, and he does. "Let's go."

Another smile crosses my lips. Whatever it takes, I remind myself.

THIRTY-FIVE

We end up driving back to the same small town where I saw the doctor several weeks ago. Josue pulls his car into the parking lot of what appears to be their fanciest restaurant in town. It's a small Italian restaurant with little white Christmas-style lights hanging from the framework. The parking lot isn't empty, but it isn't full either.

When he parks the car, he hops out immediately to run around to my side and open my door.

Cute tactic, if this was real. But none of this is real.

I kissed a boy I shouldn't have, and he kept me.

My brain tells my lips to smile, so I snap out of it and accept his outstretched hand. I stand up and walk slowly into the restaurant with him, our hands locked together. He's beaming.

"This is nice," I murmur softly.

"I'm glad you wanted to go out with me."

If I'm truly honest with myself, I rotate between angry and intrigued. I like the way that Josue's hand feels when it's holding my smaller hand, but I don't like the complete isolation on his ranch. I mostly enjoy kissing him, except when I feel like I'm reminding myself that I should be kissing him or keeping him from worrying about what I might be thinking.

We're at the entrance, and I pause for full effect. "I'll go anywhere with you," I tell him, then lean in for another kiss.

I think I'll try out for the school play some day, I think, as we enter the restaurant. All this acting experience has made me into a pro.

The hostess takes us to a booth near the back, and we sit on the same side together. I'm not sure if it's intentional, but he motions for me to take the wall seat. The table is dimly lit, and I can't see any of the other diners from where I'm seated.

It doesn't matter. It won't affect my plan.

Josue orders an appetizer; fried mushrooms with melted cheese on them. It's amazing. I've never had a mushroom that captured all its water in it, and each one feels like a million flavors being chewed at once.

I drink a full glass of water as I work through the mushrooms, and when our salads arrive, I drink another. The waitress comes back to fill my cup for a third time as the main course arrives.

We don't talk about anything significant. As I'm eating a plate of chicken alfredo, which is made with thick fettucine noodles and a white, creamy sauce, I realize that our date conversation is no different from our regular table talk. He's talking about the weather and his orchard, and I ask about when the winter frost begins. All while I finish another cup of water.

"Are you okay?" Josue asks when I stop talking all of a sudden.

"Hmm? Oh," I say. "I shouldn't have had all that water."

He chuckles. "Bathroom?"

"How did you know?" I guess I do always get quiet when I need to go to the bathroom. I've never really thought about it, but back home, I have to wait my turn for our shared bathroom.

Back home.

"Seriously, are you okay?" he asks again.

My emotions are easy to read across my face. Mami has always told me that, but I'm realizing that she's mostly right. Mostly, because I've done a phenomenal job getting us all the way to a restaurant.

"Do they have a bathroom?" I ask, glancing past him.

Josue stands, and holds out his hand again to help me up. He escorts me all the way to the bathroom door and tells me he'll wait for me.

No problem.

I go inside and lock myself into the larger stall. There's an infant changing table closed against the wall. After I go to the bathroom, I walk over to it and unlatch it. They probably clean it every night, or at least, someone will come to change a baby.

I bend down and pull the piece of paper I've had in my boot and unfold it. I wrote it earlier in the day when Josue was buying my dress and doing whatever else he does.

HELP. MY NAME IS SHAYLA RUIZ AND I'M 15 YEARS OLD. MY COYOTE WON'T TAKE ME HOME AND I AM A US CITIZEN. I AM STAYING CLOSE TO HERE AT A RANCH WITH POMEGRANATE AND ORANGE TREES. THERE ARE NO NEIGHBORS. IT'S OFF THE 98, DOWN A HIDDEN DIRT ROAD.

PLEASE CALL MY PARENTS AT #760-555-5555.

I tuck the paper into the changing table and close it, then flush the toilet and walk over to the sink. My hands are shaking, so I wash my hands a little longer than I probably need to before I walk out of the bathroom.

"Feeling better?" Josue asks.

I nod. "Yeah. My stomach was hurting a little. I'm not sure why I drank so much water."

But really, I do know why. I cringe, worried that someone will find the note before we leave.

How would Josue react?

Is he expecting me to make a run for it?

Josue must've ordered dessert while I was in the bathroom, because we each have a slice of fancy cheesecake sitting in front of us at the table. I slide back into my seat and try to enjoy the rich cake, but I keep worrying about the note.

What if nobody finds it?

And even more concerning, have I done the right thing?

***

The drive home is somber. Butterflies are fluttering in my chest, and I feel like I'm staring out the side mirror too much. But there are no other cars, so I'm looking for lights and sirens that don't exist.

"You're really quiet," Josue says.

I force a smile back onto my face. My cheeks are starting to hurt. "I'm so full," I tell him, patting my belly jokingly. "That cheesecake was amazing."

But I make an effort to talk more, especially since he took a big risk by bringing me off his property again.

"That was the first Italian restaurant I've ever been to. I've had spaghetti and pizza before, but never real Italian food. I liked it."

"It was pretty good."

Oh, I probably need to talk about more than food. I let my eyes wander back to him; away from the road. "Well, I've survived my first date ever."

Josue's eyes light up. "I would love a million more dates with you."

I don't say the words that I've learned not to say. Instead, I settle for safe words. "Tell me about the best restaurant you've ever been to."

We spend the rest of the ride home talking about fancy food and places he's been. I'm admittedly very limited in my experiences, since I've been a poor girl in Calexico my whole life, but it's kind of fun to hear about the world from him. I didn't know that he used to live in Texas, and he's got stories about restaurants and exciting places that I've never considered before.

By the time we arrive back at the ranch, I feel calm again. My hands aren't trembling, and I can pretend that I haven't just told on him. But I did leave a note, and I'm hopeful that someone will find it.

Josue finds a deck of cards and we play the only card game we both know for a few hours – Go Fish. He lets me win, which would be cute if I didn't feel trapped here. Instead, I smile at him and wait for his cue to go to bed.

After I remove my boot and he tucks me in, I turn towards him and shove a protective pillow between us. "Thanks for tonight," I tell him.

I can't see him in the dark, but I can feel his smile. Is that how it is for older couples?

I guess I won't know, because this isn't real. And I'm going to find my way home.

"Good night, *mi amor*," Josue whispers. I close my eyes and feign sleep. I'm not ready for that conversation yet.

THIRTY-SIX

The following morning, we're sitting on the porch again, and I'm watching a gentle breeze pass through the orchard. I'm at one end of the swing, and Josue is at the other end. My ankle has been starting to swell again, so I'm half sitting, half lying on the swing, with my legs propped across a pillow. Josue is seated next to the pillow, and he's awkwardly holding an ice pack over my foot.

"Can I call my parents?" I ask. I wasn't brave enough to ask before our "date," but now I've done what I needed to do. This morning, I woke up with a heaviness in my heart and I feel like I need to ask him everything I've never dared to wonder aloud.

Josue shakes his head slowly. "I'm not ready for you to go yet."

I'm starting to wonder if he'll ever be ready. I glance over at the dreadful building in his backyard. "Have you ever kept someone before?" I suddenly ask.

His hand freezes over my foot and he stares up at me with a serious expression on his face. "Shayla," he tells me. "I promise you that I've never gotten close to any of them. I've never kept anyone else."

"Then, why me?" I ask.

He shifts the ice pack to the side of my ankle and looks away. "You're special," he says finally.

"But why? How am I special?" I ask. Seriously, I don't understand. No boy has ever looked at me the way that Josue looks at me. His eyes always look so focused, like he's memorizing every inch of me.

"You're kind. Sweet. Funny," he says. He turns his head back in my direction to look at me. "You're beautiful."

I feel my cheeks growing warm, and that reckless feeling flickers from my fingertips and up my arms. I try to see myself the way that he sees me; but I've always just seen myself as a dutiful kid who would do anything to please my parents. I work hard, study hard, run hard. I've never really tried to figure out who I am underneath all my actions.

"Shayla, let's go for a walk," he offers.

I point to my foot. "I'll carry you," he offers.

"That probably isn't a good idea," I say. He smiles. I feel like he's too in tune with me, and he can tell that I'm losing my senses around him. I watch as he slowly places the boot back over my ankle and affixes the velcro straps.

Once my boot is back on, I stand up and stretch my arms. We've been on the swing for hours. But my foot still hurts, and I really don't want to walk on it.

"What do you think?" he asks once he's standing up next to me.

I shrug. I've run out of ways to say "No" to this man, and that terrifies me. "Whatever."

Josue wraps his arm around my back and catches me with his other hand. It reminds me of those television shows when a groom carries his bride after a wedding. I frown. That's not what this is.

His arm is sturdy under my back, but I feel like I'm falling. I reach up and place my hands around his neck, which inadvertently brings our faces closer together.

I immediately turn away. This isn't right.

Two weeks ago, I hated him.

Three weeks ago, I tried to escape from him at the border.

Four weeks ago, I didn't even know him.

Before that, I was home with my parents.

"Josue, if you really care about me, you'll take me home," I finally say. He looks away, his gaze somewhere in the distance. "I can still be your girlfriend."

He sets me down.

"Fine. Can I take a walk?"

"Alone?"

"Yes, Josue. Alone. I'll go pick a pomegranate and walk back."

He considers this, and then nods. "Maybe the fresh air will make you feel better."

"Maybe."

THIRTY-SEVEN

When I reach the small grove of fruit trees, I pause in front of the first pomegranate tree. The fruit are up too high.

I turn around, and I can see Josue still standing on the porch. He's watching me. I wave. He really doesn't need to be so worried. It's not like I'm going to make a run for it.

If I was going to do that, I would've run last night from the restaurant.

My note. I wonder if anyone's found it.

I trudge onward, a shock of pain running up my leg. My ankle is sore from walking too much yesterday. At the fourth tree, I reach up and pick a pomegranate. The flesh is soft, and I immediately rip it into two large pieces. The seeds are red and juicy, like blood dripping from a gaping wound.

I'm not sure why I did that. My hands are immediately sticky from the sugary syrup, and I wasn't planning to eat it out here. But when I look back, I see Josue standing in the middle of the field, holding something. He's shouting, but I don't understand what he's saying.

From three trees away, someone calls my name. "Shayla Ruiz?"

I snap my attention towards the voice. A woman is standing behind the tree, wearing a navy-blue jacket with yellow letters that say FBI.

Oh, no.

I whip around, realizing too late that the thing in Josue's hand is a gun. Just as several agents rush past me, guns drawn. "Drop the weapon!" one of them yells.

"Come with me," the lady tells me. She's suddenly beside me, dragging me away from whatever is happening to Josue.

"Josue!" I scream, just as a ricochet of bullets are released in his direction.

My feet launch forward in a sprint I've known my whole life. His body is falling, falling, falling. Dropping to the ground, as I'm running across the field. Pain screams up my leg and I push onward. Red juice from a forgotten pomegranate muddies my fingers as I hurry towards what I already know to be true.

When I reach his body, I already know.

He's gone.

***

I've never seen a dead man before. And Josue is so much more than that. I can feel their arms clawing at me, pulling me away. But some animal instinct that I have just realized lives inside of me has roared to life, and I'm on my knees clutching him. They're pulling me back, and I'm trying to hold on.

"No, no, no," I moan. "This wasn't supposed to happen. You can't just leave," I whisper. My voice is thick, and the words sound older, more pained than I knew I could speak. "Get up," I demand.

His lifeless body does nothing. His head is turned towards me, and those eyes that used to only look at me are now staring off into the distance. Unfocused.

"Josue," I cry as they finally pry me off him. His body isn't warm anymore. His skin is rigid, like a giant piece of clay that has been molded into shape and left out in the sun for too long.

I'm lifted backwards, into a standing position. Strong arms are pulling me away, making my feet walk five, ten, twenty yards away from him.

My note did this. I did this.

"Are you Shayla Ruiz?" a woman asks me. I stare at her blankly. Her face is plain, and she has blonde hair tied back in a fierce bun. Brownish eyes, a few freckles along her cheeks. She's wearing one of the FBI windbreakers too.

I open my mouth to speak, but nothing comes out. I try again, but nothing. I turn back to the field where Josue's body awaits. There are several agents, circling him with cameras and writing insignificant things into little notepads that they hold in their hands.

"Shayla," the woman says. My hands are shaking and when I glance down to try to convince myself that I can control their movements, I see the violent smear of blood across my chest. The mixture of pomegranate juice intertwined with fresh blood on my fingers.

Josue's blood.

Everything goes dark after that.

THIRTY-EIGHT

"It's okay," someone is saying. "You're safe now."

I'm lying on some sort of thick surface. I try to move but my arms have something heavy on them. My eyelids feel heavy, like I'm pushing myself out of some dark place. It takes several long minutes before I'm able to open my eyes.

And there are several people standing over me. It takes me a moment to recognize the woman who had tried to talk to me in Josue's yard. The FBI lady. Next to her is another officer, a guy, and a paramedic. I'm lying on a gurney in the back of an ambulance.

"What happened?" I ask frantically. "Where are you taking me?" My voice is heavy, my throat hoarse. I could drink a gallon of water right now, if they would let me.

"Shayla, you fainted," the woman says. She makes an effort to scrunch up her face into what she probably assumes is a friendly smile. It isn't.

I close my eyes shut, willing the day to scramble into reverse. Before the gunshots, before the agents grabbed me. If only I could go back in time and reverse all of this. Reverse last night.

There's a siren blaring overhead, but it feels like it's in another place. Far away. I feel my heartbeat catching up with the rhythmic swaying of the ambulance as we rush forward. Not in reverse, not where I need to go.

"Is he...?" I ask. I can't say it. I can't believe this thing has happened. My eyes flicker open and I train them on the male agent.

He grimaces. "He's gone."

The hot sting of tears begins to leak from the edges of my face. Crying is the worst when a person is lying down flat. I feel them drizzling downwards, over my cheeks and into my ears. A useless little pool of hot saline, really.

I've cried so many tears. Like a lifetime of tears, in just a few months.

The ambulance grinds to a halt and I feel everything shift. The siren stops screaming over me, and the back door is yanked open from the outside. I'm moving, being lifted up and then pulled downward. A metal clanging sound underneath the gurney tells me that the wheels have been locked into place. They wheel me inward; away from crisp air and into an artificially bright room. All the while, the two officers and now two male paramedics hover over me.

"We need a private room," I hear the woman telling someone. I close my eyes and wait for whatever comes next.

"Do you have any injuries that I need to know about?" the man in the long white coat is asking me. I'm in a small room in the emergency department of a hospital in the middle of nowhere. I've never even been in a hospital before, well, at least not since I was born. I am seated somewhat upright and staring at the doctor anxiously. Someone stands beside him, jotting down notes. Their plastic badge on their scrubs says "scribe." I'm not quite sure what that means, but at least the man with the white coat has a clearly defined role. His says that his name is Dr. Williams, and his badge says "physician" in large letters. I know who he is.

I glance at both agents. They have stayed by my side, even though the paramedics quickly left. They don't wear badges. Their dark jackets scream "FBI" in bold yellow letters on the back. The woman has maintained a bit of a scowl on her plain features. The man is tall and has tan skin. His build is strong, brave. He seems a bit tense but has made an effort to smile in my direction a few times. I glance back at the physician and say nothing.

Dr. Williams nods slowly, then stares at the two officers. "I will need some privacy to interview my patient," he declares.

I keep my eyes focused on his face. Cocoa skin, dark eyes. Short black hair. He has fatherly eyes, and something about the way that he's already demanded privacy reminds me of my Papi. I wait while the two agents leave the room.

When the doctor and his scribe are alone with me in the room, I fold my arms over my chest and ask, "What is going to happen to me?"

The scribe pauses his pen and stops writing, as the physician takes the small rolling chair next to me and sits. He levels his head and stares directly into my eyes. "We have to examine you, to make sure you're safe," he says. "And then, we have to examine you for evidence."

"Evidence?" I ask. The word sounds hollow, broken as it slips out of my mouth.

"There's a forensics doctor that will come and do the second part of the exam," he says softly. "But for now, tell me what hurts."

I bite my lip and point to my foot. "I have an ankle fracture," I say. "A bit of something called the fibula." My mind flashes back to the urgent care, when Josue asked the doctor about my ankle. His eyes looked so worried. So kind.

So dead.

I snap my attention back to Dr. Williams. He's asking me something. I didn't hear him, so I raise an eyebrow and wait for him to repeat himself. "How did it happen?" he asks. His words are calm, patient. Like he's met girls like me all the time.

"I fell when we were crossing the border," I say. "I got scared, and everything was dark."

"When was that?" he asks.

"A while ago. Maybe three weeks?" I offer.

He nods. The scribe writes down my answer on his clipboard. "And when did you get that boot?"

My fingers automatically reach for the tall edge of the boot. I trace them along the rim. "About a week after," I say, staring down at the dark material. Josue's hand reaching for mine slips into my memory, and suddenly all the nerve endings in my hand feel numb. I stretch my fingers, trying to regain my feeling. "I thought it was a sprain, but I still couldn't walk on it. So, he took me to the doctor."

"I see," he says. The "he" is obvious, I guess. Everyone must've heard about the shootout.

"What does forensics mean?" I ask.

Dr. Williams sighs. His forehead is crinkled, and I realize that he's probably older than my Papi. "It means that the officers are requesting a pelvic exam. Did that man hurt you?"

"He was kind to me."

"You're a victim," the physician tells me.

I shake my head. "He didn't do anything to me." I can feel my anger rising. Josue didn't hurt me. He took me to a doctor. He fed me. He kept me safe. He brought me back to the United States when my own country stranded me in Mexico.

And he didn't let me go. He wanted me to stay with him forever.

I told him I was his girlfriend. I'm the one that kissed him first.

Or was I?

"Sometimes, when you're held in captivity, you might develop a sense of closeness with your kidnapper," the doctor says.

I sit upright and glare at him. "I wasn't kidnapped."

He stares back at me, eyes wide. "And you weren't free. I saw the news. Your parents paid, and you weren't released."

I glance back at the door; the same door that the officers left through. They aren't behind me. I turn my head back to face Dr. Williams. "The news?" I ask, fear creeping back into my words.

"Your parents were on the news, begging for your release," he says.

I bow my head down in shame. They were worried about me. Mami. Papi. Brenden. Esteban. My friends, my teachers. The people at the diner. Everyone.

People I didn't even know were worried about me.

And I was sitting in Josue's house, imagining something different. I dared myself to even consider a possible future with him. To imagine living at his ranch with my parents and my younger brothers.

I close my eyes and release all the tears I have left within me. I feel my body swaying somewhat, and my stomach aches. The grief of loss versus the pain of what I've done to everyone I love. I can't even imagine how badly my parents have missed me, and since Josue got shot, I haven't even thought once about them.

"I need my Mami," I whisper.

"I'm sorry, Shayla," the doctor's voice says. "You're in federal custody, so I don't get to make that decision."

My eyes flutter open and I stare at him again. "What do I need to do?" I ask.

He nods and brings in a forensics nurse. Together, they begin taking photos of me and examine every inch of my body.

THIRTY-NINE

Too many hours pass, and then I'm released. There was a forensics doctor, and they collected swabs and took pictures of parts of my body that I've never showed to anyone. The cold room and exam table have made me feel exposed.

My ankle has been x-rayed again, and I've listened to advice and taken a handful of pills "to prevent infection or unwanted pregnancy." Even though I've shouted that I'm still a virgin, no one is hearing me. All they know is that I cried when I saw Josue's lifeless body on the ground, and based on where they just examined me, they clearly didn't believe me. I protested, but eventually just closed my eyes and tried to imagine I was somewhere else. I realized that I'm too tired to fight.

When I'm finally allowed to leave the emergency room, a nurse I have barely met wheels me out to an awaiting black sedan with another agent in the driver's seat. My two federal agents flank me on either side, and I wait for the wheelchair to park before I take a tentative step forward.

Pain jolts up my leg. My desperate dash towards Josue is going to set me back some on my recovery. And it changed nothing.

"Watch your step," the nurse says softly. I'm apparently a bit of a celebrity, according to what the last nurse had told me. This one seems nonplussed, but still, there was a strange silence in the air as I was wheeled out of a busy, loud emergency room.

My parents went on TV to ask for my safe return. My private, terrified parents. The same two people who are terrified of the authorities and would do anything to keep themselves out of public sight. They exposed themselves, for me.

The agents had confirmed for me that my Papi was the one who called the FBI. They waited three days after they paid before he called. By then, the calls from Josue had stopped, and he knew that I wasn't coming home unless he did something.

That must've been why he was staring at his phone. I've been all over the news, and I had no idea.

But he did.

No wonder he blocked me into the corner at the restaurant when we went on our first date. Only date, I correct myself. But so many things are suddenly making sense to me.

Once I'm seated in the back seat next to the guy agent, I tilt my head in his direction. "When can I go home?" I ask.

He smiles, that faint trace of kindness flashing across his face again. "We have some questions for you, and then we'll get you back to your parents."

"Fine," I say.

The ride is long, and I watch through the window as we trace our way westward, towards San Diego. The large city spreads out in front of me, and we finally reach our destination. The car pulls underground, into a basement garage underneath a formidable building with walls of tall glass windows. They're the kind that you can probably only see outwards from, like a whole building made up of one-way glass.

When the car parks, I wait for the female agent to open my door for me. It has those awkward child locks on it, so I can't get out on my own.

I walk slowly between the two of them, with the driver leading the way ahead of us. A small army of FBI agents to escort me through a labyrinth of small corridors towards an elevator. They enter the elevator with me, and our driver presses the button for the eighth floor. I lean back against the wall of the elevator as it lifts us upwards away from land. I've never been in a tall building before, and I feel myself swaying as the ground moves underneath me.

"Shayla," the female agent says, grabbing my arm. "No more fainting, okay? We don't need another ER visit tonight."

I nod and force myself to keep my eyes open. No more fainting.

The elevator comes to a stop and the doors jolt open. I let the lady pull me forwards, away from the small rectangular trap that carried us up to the eighth floor. We walk through a series of cubicles and down another long corridor before they take me to a small room at the end of the hallway. It's another interrogation room, and this time, they're not making me wait for the rapid-fire question and answer session.

I take my seat at the table, the one facing the long glass window that surely leads to somewhere else. The two agents who went with me to the hospital sit across from me, and the driver hovers over them.

"Alright, Shayla," the driver says. It's the first time I've heard his voice, and it booms over me. Loud and sturdy. "Tell us where you've been for the past month."

My head is buzzing. Has it really been a month? I set my hands on the table and start fidgeting with my fingernails. They're nicely trimmed now; Josue brought me his pair of nail clippers when I finally asked for them.

I close my eyes and try to figure out where to begin. In the end, they control where the story goes, and I answer each one of their questions as succinctly as possible.

Yes, I was deported. No, I shouldn't have been. Yes, I went to Tijuana. I met some people who told me to go east. I went to Tecate. I met Josue in a park. Yes, he let me stay in his house. No, I don't remember where it was. No, there weren't any other people with us. No, he didn't go back to Mexico after he brought me to the US. Yes, he took my parents' money. No, he didn't release me.

No, I don't think he was working with anyone else. I never saw any other girls. Well, yeah, maybe someone did pick up the money from my parents, but I don't actually know who. What? Trafficking victims? He had a shed in the back, a dark, dark room with beds...

Finally, they ask the question that I know I don't want to answer.

"Why do you need to know?" I ask. I stare into each of their eyes, waiting for some response that lets me know that they're human, like me. "What does it matter? He's dead."

"Did he do anything to you?" the woman asks.

I shake my head. Perhaps too quickly.

"There's something that happens when people are kept in captivity. It's called Stockholm syndrome," she starts to explain.

All we did was kiss. Too much.

I tune her out. Dr. Williams had given me the same speech, and I heard a bit more from the forensics nurse who took all those samples and looked *down there*. I don't want to continue this conversation.

"Are we finished yet?" I cross my arms more tightly over my chest, waiting for the moment to pass. I am almost on the verge of tears, and I've cried too much. My heart is heavy, and I need to see my parents.

The agents wait for several long minutes. None of us speak. Finally, the door behind me opens slightly, and someone must've signaled them or something because the woman sighs heavily and the man with the almost kind smile says, "Your mother is here to pick you up."

***

"I'm sorry, Mami," I murmur as she hurries into the little interrogation room. My body aches to hug her, but I hold my arms steadily across my chest instead. Not here, not in this place with these people. The federal agents who have been interrogating me for the last several hours are scrutinizing my every move.

She glances down at my leg, where the walking boot screams of my broken ankle.

"What did he do to you?" she asks, pausing in the middle of the room.

I close my eyes and recall the words of the officer had told me. "Stockholm syndrome," buzzes through my brain.

"I'm okay," I lie. She's standing close enough to hug me, but not wrapping her arms around me. That look in her eye; the one that she uses when she's ready to reprimand one of us. Or when one of the customers at the diner said something inappropriate to her. "I'll be okay," I add.

An awkward silence passes between us. How long have I been gone? And how did everything change so fast?

"Patricia's cousin drove me here. Let's get you home," she says.

The agents don't stop her when she grabs my arm and directs me out of the room. I follow behind her like a small child, hobbling slowly on my bad ankle.

I am anything but a small child. Josue's face flashes through my brain and my mom's grasp on my wrist burns. We're almost out of the building so I accept the pain.

PART FOUR
HOME

FORTY

"Shayla Ruiz!" a woman calls out. She's standing in front of our trailer with a microphone, and there's several other people around her. A man stands near her, holding one of those bulky cameras. Several lights flash at the same time. Mami grabs my arm and pulls me back inside.

The door is quickly closed and bolted shut. I turn to face my family, not sure how to fix this mess. "I'm so sorry," I say. Papi is sitting at the dining room table, staring blankly at the television. My face is flashed across the screen, followed by Josue's, then a wide angle shot of his ranch.

My heart hurts. I can't believe he's gone.

He was the most broken human I've ever met.

And I'm scared that I might've fallen in love with him. If that was love. I'm not sure I'll ever know.

Mami engulfs me in a fierce hug. She's smaller than me, but her arms are confident and graceful. Brenden and Esteban are hovering behind her, watching me with wide eyes.

"*Mija, no llores.*" That's the weirdest part. Mami is talking in Spanish to me all of a sudden. I don't understand everything that she says, but parts of it are making sense to me.

I did not realize that I was crying until she told me to stop. I swipe my hand across my face, trying to stem the flow of tears. In all my life, I've never cried as much as I have over the past two months.

Josue. The first man I've ever kissed.

Mami knows. I don't know if she will tell Papi. But I'm pretty sure she figured out that I kissed Josue. I worry that she thinks I did more than that. But no one is asking. In fact, no one wants to know anything about Josue.

Someone knocks on the door, stealing away the moment. Mami drops her arms and I walk to the doorway. "Shayla, no," she says.

"It's okay, Mami," I tell her. I'm not the same girl that I was just a few months ago. There's a heavy weight hanging down on my shoulders. The weight of loss. I've lost so much. The normalcy of being a regular kid. Time. Josue.

I can't believe this is happening. After everything that had already happened, and now we have a media circus in front of our freaking trailer park.

I peek through the curtain and see a woman in a stylish business suit. She does not have a microphone in her hand; rather, she is carrying a black briefcase. I unlock the door and open it a few inches.

"Hi," I say nervously.

The woman flashes me a perfect smile. "Shayla Ruiz, I am so glad to meet you," she says, reaching out her hand. I don't reciprocate, so she lowers her hand. Her smile doesn't falter for even a second. "Right. I'm Lilia Marquez, and I'm a human rights attorney. I'd like to represent you and your family. For free." She flashes her smile in my parents' direction as well.

"Why do I need to be represented?" I ask. I feel Mami's hand on my shoulder.

"Oh. I figured you had been notified," she says. "They announced on the news already, but your parents are going to receive an order of deportation." Briefly, her lips flatten, but then she smiles again. "I'd like to help your family," she says.

I am holding the edge of the doorway with my hand, and I feel my fingers starting to tremble. "Why?" I ask.

"I'm guessing that the Border Patrol is under a lot of scrutiny for wrongfully deporting you, so perhaps the Immigration officials decided to go after your parents," she says.

I shake my head. "But why do you want to help?"

Mami gasps. "Shayla," she says loudly. I feel her reaching for my arm, but I move forward.

"No, Mami," I say, ignoring Mami's shock. "Seriously, why?" I ask again.

Ms. Lilia Marquez is still smiling. It's unnerving. "I believe in justice," she says.

I nod slowly. "Come in," I say softly, backing away from the door. She passes quickly through the doorway and Papi closes the door behind her.

I'll give her some credit for not acting like our living room is too poor for her. She waits for a moment until Papi offers for her to sit at our dining room table, and all of us follow her. Mami rushes to the kitchen to make a fresh pot of coffee.

"How are you holding up?" she asks me. Her expression is serious, and her smile fades for the moment. I'm actually glad that she decided to stop smiling.

"I'll be okay," I say. Because it's true, I will be okay eventually. But right now, I'm the furthest thing from okay. Every time I close my eyes, I see Josue's body falling to the ground. I hear the sound of bullets ricocheting through the air. Why did he have a gun?

Did he always have a gun?

How hadn't I noticed?

FORTY-ONE

As much as I wish for normalcy, normal never comes. I enter my old high school several days later, and suddenly everyone knows my name. I was recognizable as a member of the cross-country team before, but now I'm "Shayla Ruiz, the girl who was kidnapped" or "Shayla, the girl from the news."

I try to settle into my first period seat, but there's commotion all around me. In ninth grade, I had two close friends and I was nice to everyone. But I don't see either Emma or Marla. Instead, I'm trying to pretend my life hasn't been flipped upside down, but there's no denying it. Everyone is stealing glances in my direction, and the tall kid next to me isn't even trying to hide the way he's staring at me.

Courtney, one of the junior varsity cheerleaders, smiles sweetly at me from in front of the tall kid. "*Bienvenidos*," she says in a terrible white girl accent. It comes out choppy, like Being-veng-ee-dohs.

"I'm from here."

I don't want to have all this attention. I just want to be a regular kid from a happy home, working my way towards a college scholarship. But I can't do that with all these kids staring at me.

It gets worse as the day rolls onward. I see Emma across the hallway when I'm trying to make it to Mr. Porter's English class. I wave shyly, and she looks like she wants to say something to me, but suddenly four popular girls jump in between where she's standing and where I'm at.

"I heard you shot him," the tallest girl says. I remember her from the school play last year. She's a fiery senior with a whole lot of attitude. Delilah Chaves.

I shake my head quickly, trying to erase the image of Josue's body laying on the ground. So completely still. I can still smell the heavy scent of gunfire mixed with the fragrant scent of pomegranates.

"I need to get to class," I say, trying to push past them. I look over Delilah's shoulder, but I don't see Emma anymore. The bell rings, indicating that I'm already running late to my second class of the day. My ankle feels heavy from all the walking, or probably more from when I ran across the field after Josue was shot.

"Right. So now you're worried about your grades and stuff?" Margo Jimenez says before she blows a rather flimsy balloon from her bubble gum. Margo Jimenez has never, ever spoken to me before.

When I finally succeed in slipping away from the girls, I race down an almost empty hall to English.

"*Hablas inglés?*" Patrick asks as I hurry into the room.

Mr. Porter is one of the teacher volunteers at home meets, so he knows me already. I force a fake smile on my face as I stumble past all the seated students and hand him my schedule.

"It's my first day," I tell him.

He nods. "Welcome back, Shayla," he answers me in a low voice. "Let me know if you need anything. The counselor is also planning to chat with you."

I shrug and glance around the room, looking for an empty seat.

And there's only one.

Right next to Patrick, the jerk who just asked if I speak English.

As if I haven't been going to school with most of these kids for my entire life.

By the end of the day, one thing is certain. I am not the same girl who went for a run a little over a month ago. It started with La Migra, but Josue was the one who changed me. Or maybe, I allowed myself to change in ways I hadn't even considered.

I don't think I can manage another seven months of tenth grade.

*****

Mami is probably the smartest woman in the whole United States. When I leave class and begin my slow walk home, she's already standing on the corner waiting for me.

213

I try to raise my shoulders up just a little bit, so she won't worry about me quite so much. But the stoic look on her face tells me she knows everything.

"Hi, Mami," I tell her when I reach the corner. She immediately reaches for my backpack and places it on her own back. I don't even try to stop her. She's small, but sturdy.

"Ay, *Miel.* It was that bad?"

"Yeah."

We begin walking in silence. My leg is sore from racing all over high school, and I wish I could soak my foot in Josue's large bathtub for the next several hours.

But I'm not at his large ranch house anymore. We reach the small trailer and I have to suck in a deep breath to tamper down another flood of emotions.

I can't believe I miss him so much.

And I can't believe how guilty I feel about not missing my family enough. "I'm sorry, Mami," I tell her for what is probably the thousandth time.

She doesn't respond.

As Mami unlatches the front door, a sedan pulls up in front of our tiny home. Our lawyer climbs out of the passenger seat and smooths imaginary wrinkles from her skirt.

Mami waves at her, but I can't stand on my sore ankle anymore. I duck into the doorway and move as quickly as my foot will allow, until I'm at the sofa. I sink into the thin cushions and try not to imagine that barren house in Tecate with Frida's odd painting.

How had I missed the fact that he had a gun?

What else didn't I know?

Probably everything.

Lilia Marquez and Mami enter the trailer, and Mami casts a sad look in my direction. She sees that I've already propped my foot up on the sofa, and I immediately lower it. "Sorry."

It's my new favorite word.

All I do is hurt people now.

"How was school?" Lilia Marquez asks.

I study our lawyer. She's wearing another suit, but this time it's navy blue and she's got a fancy string of pearls around her neck. She is hovering near our ancient sofa, but not seated. It's weird though. She doesn't seem completely uncomfortable in our tiny rented trailer.

"Okay," I lie. Mami stares at me for a moment, so I shake my head. "Actually, it was awful. Everyone was treating me like I was someone different. I didn't like it."

"Well," Lilia Marquez says. I'm really not sure if I think of her as Lilia or Ms. Marquez yet. "Hopefully that sorts itself out. For now, we need to talk."

Mami offers our lawyer a seat, and she sits across from me on the mismatched orange sofa chair. It doesn't recline. My mind is immediately drawn back to Josue's little house in Tecate, with the reclining chair and strange painting.

And his gun. Of course, he had a gun. He was an international smuggler. A coyote.

But he was also Josue.

Mami tucks herself underneath my outstretched leg at the other end of the sofa and stares at Lilia Marquez expectantly.

"ICE has come to a decision in your case," she says, pulling a folder out of her large purse. I watch as she flips it open and hands Mami a letter printed on fancy paper. There's an official seal stamped in the corner.

"What does it say?"

Mami's mouth forms a little shocked "O" shape, and she hands the paper to me.

"Notice of Deportation."

My hand instantly jerks up to cover my own mouth as a cascade of tears unleashes down my face. "What?" I scan the page further, and there are three names.

Papi.

Mami.

Me.

"Why?" I ask, my finger tracing my name on the official document.

Lilia Marquez sighs. "You signed a form for deportation when you were arrested."

"But I'm a US citizen."

"Apparently, you gave up that right when you signed."

When I glance over at Mami, I see that tears are raining down her cheeks, as well. I can't think of the last time I saw Mami cry before all this mess.

"But I'm fifteen."

"Doesn't matter. This administration takes two-year olds to court."

I shake my head. "It should matter. It should."

Mami coughs twice, then clears her throat. "Shayla is right. It should matter. What can we do?"

"I'd like for you to speak to the press," Lilia Marquez says. "I have an offer for you to speak on one of the early morning television shows. Wake Up, USA."

"Wake Up, USA?" I ask. It's national, and it has several fancy people in business suits announcing the news and asking Americans to care about whatever pressing issues are occurring in the United States. Sometimes, it talks about world events, but more often, it focuses on homegrown issues.

"No," Mami says, just as I say, "I'll do it."

We glance at each other. She shakes her head.

"Mami, I know you want to protect me," I say. "And I hate that all of this happened. But I have to try."

"When do we have to leave?" Mami asks, bringing my attention back to the Deportation Order in my hands. I glance down at it, seeing the date highlighted at the bottom.

One week.

"What about my brothers?"

Our lawyer doesn't hesitate. "They can stay in foster care, or they can go with you."

"Can we fight this?"

"It's almost impossible to get it reversed under the current administration. But we can file a suit against Border Patrol for what they did." She looks directly at me, her eyes locked on my face. "We should file suit."

I nod. "Yes, to both, then. Yes, we need a lawsuit. And yes, I'll talk to whoever you want me to talk to."

FORTY-TWO

"Welcome to Wake Up, USA!" the hostess, Darlene Tomkins says as she smiles into the camera on the screen in front of me.

A film crew has set themselves up in our tiny living room. Lilia Marquez accessorized our trailer for us yesterday afternoon, and there's suddenly a surplus of throw pillows and soft blankets stretched across the sofa to cover our poverty. The photos on the wall have all been reframed, and there's a brand-new family photo collage filled with our happiest childhood pics.

And there aren't many pictures to choose from. We have school photos and a few pictures that I was able to collect from Emma. She came over after Lilia Marquez left yesterday. Everything happened so fast after that.

Mami is dressed in a simple blue blouse with her apron over it. Papi is seated next to her in a button-down grey shirt. His hair has started to fade into the same color as his shirt.

"Good morning, Shayla," Darlene says, her smile cheerier than I'm comfortable with. Nothing feels good about this morning, with a deportation order counting down our days left in the U.S.

"Hi."

"Everyone, this is Shayla Ruiz, the girl that we were searching for in the Southern California desert. She's here to tell us about her journey," the hostess states directly into the camera, then turns back to look at me. "Shayla, can you introduce your family to us?"

I smile politely. Ms. Lilia Marquez was very clear with me. We need to gain the sympathy of the general public, or no one will stand with us. "Of course. This is my mother, and this is my father," I say, pointing in their direction. My Mami smiles nervously for the camera. Papi doesn't share her expression. He looks concerned.

"And these are my little brothers, Esteban and Brenden."

Brenden waves cheerfully at the camera. He thinks it's really cool that we'll be on tv. Esteban grins, but then leans against Mami for support.

They're all seated together on the blanket-wrapped sofa, and I'm sitting next to them on a chair from the kitchen.

"Shayla, everyone wants to know how you ended up at that desert ranch. Can you tell us a little about that?"

I swallow hard. The long walk from Tijuana to Tecate floods my memories, and I cringe without meaning to. Ms. Lilia Marquez is standing off camera, and her face is stern.

Right. Answer the question I wanted them to ask, not necessarily the one that they asked me. She prepped me for this interview.

"I was running, not too far from here. Before all of this happened, I was trying to earn a college scholarship for cross country." I pause dramatically, glancing down at my large boot. The camera obediently follows and captures my injury before shifting back to my face.

"For cross country, we run in all terrains, and I liked to practice in the mountains. On that day, when I was running through the mountains, and I ran right into an area where Border Patrol was arresting a group of migrants."

Ms. Lilia Marquez nods her head. "And they pointed their guns at me and made me drop to the ground. One of the officers stepped on me with his boot, even though I did everything they said."

"That sounds awful," the hostess says.

"It was, Ms. Tomkins," I tell her, nodding my head.

She blushes. "You can call me Darlene."

"Thanks, Darlene." I turn my head back towards the camera. Back to all the viewers, including the teens who have been posting the hashtag #SaveShayla all over the internet. The ones who have been following our story closely. "They took me to a detention facility, but they kept me separate from everyone else."

"Why do you think they did that?"

I sigh. "I don't speak Spanish. They didn't believe me when I told them I was born here." I reach into a small manila folder that I've had tucked next to me beside my chair and pull out a piece of paper, which I hold up for the camera to zoom in on. My birth certificate.

"I was born here, in El Centro. I am an American."

"And then what happened?"

"They deported me to Tijuana, Mexico." I pause, then glance at my Mami, who is now quietly crying. We've already agreed that I won't say that she told me to agree to be deported.

Darlene's eyes widen as I continue speaking. "I'm fifteen. I was in my track suit. I didn't have any money or identification with me, I don't speak Spanish, and my family isn't from Mexico. But they left me in Tijuana."

"Is that where you met the Coyote?"

I shake my head. "No. Tijuana was dangerous. A scary man started following me, so I hid. A girl told me that people get trafficked there. She told me to go east, to Tecate. So, I did."

"How did you get there?"

"I walked. It took several days. I was scared, starving, and dirty by the time I got to Tecate. And when I sat down to rest, Josue… the Coyote… found me."

A hushed silence settles across the room. Everyone is lingering on my words. I take another deep breath before I continue.

"The Coyote offered me a way home. And I was in a foreign country. Remember, I'm fifteen. So, I agreed." I glance at my parents, who are both nodding slowly. "He took me to his house, and I stayed there for around a week before we crossed into the US."

I pause, adjusting my ankle. It's been throbbing for days. Running was a mistake.

"But I was scared, and when we crossed into the US, I was really jumpy, so I tripped and twisted my ankle. It turns out that I broke it."

Darlene is a reporter, and she caught what I hadn't said before I could move on. "You couldn't walk? How did you cross?"

"He carried me."

The camera fixates on my face. I don't know what emotion to try to share with the audience, so I keep my face as stone cold as I can. I don't think I was supposed to answer that question, because Ms. Lilia Marquez is shaking her head.

"Were you romantically involved with your Coyote? What was his name, Josue?"

I shake my head quickly, trying not to remember the feel of his arms around mine. The way he carried me when I couldn't walk. The way he took me on my first date, and how amazing chicken alfredo with cheesecake was.

"He didn't let me come home to my family."

"But he didn't treat you badly?"

I shrug. "I couldn't walk, so I wasn't a threat. After I got the boot, he did put me in the back building overnight."

"The back building?"

"The place where he usually kept migrants."

"So where was he keeping you, that was different from the other migrants?"

I freeze. Oh my God. This hostess is a true reporter. She's taking me down paths I don't want to go down. My lawyer is shaking her head fiercely.

"I begged him to bring me home."

"Let's go back a little. You said, 'After you got the boot.' Did he take you to the doctor?"

I nod slowly. "I couldn't walk."

"But he's a Coyote. Why did he care?"

I'm starting to get mad. This has nothing to do with our case, and I feel like I'm on trial. "I don't know. The FBI shot him, so I guess we'll never be able to ask him."

"About that. Did you know he had a gun?"

I shake my head, but tears are already streaming down my cheeks.

Ms. Lilia Marquez walks over to stand beside me, facing the live studio audience. "My client still needs therapy to cope with all the trauma from her ordeal. It's all still quite vivid." She pats me on my shoulder, but the feeling of her cold hand startles me.

"The bigger issue here is that the US deported a fifteen year old child who is a US citizen to a country that she has no ties to, and now that she made it home, they're maintaining her order of deportation because she signed under duress, without counsel, an order of deportation. And they're deporting her parents."

"That's awful," the hostess says.

I nod. The cameraman zooms in on my face. I've got ugly tears making rivers and streams down my cheeks, and my nose feels wet. I'm afraid to wipe it away on national tv, so I just stare down at my lap.

"All I ever wanted was to be a good student and earn a scholarship to college. I wanted to be here with my parents. I've done everything that's ever been asked of me. I've never asked for anything, but right now, I need to ask for one thing." I lift my head up, ready to accept that this is the face that America will see. "Please, let us stay. My parents are good people, and I'm just a kid. I'm fifteen. I'm a straight A student and I have never gotten into trouble before. Please."

Darlene thanks me, the interview ends, and the camera crew begins to clean up. I sit completely still on my chair.

I've never been so humiliated.

In a million years, I never would have expected that I would have to beg for my legal right to stay in my own country, on national television, with tears and mucus all over my face.

"Thanks, Shayla," Darlene says before she leaves. I mutter something, then bury my face in my hands.

If I didn't have a broken ankle, bulky boot, and sadness emanating from every molecule of my body, I'd stand bravely. But instead, I cry.

I think I've earned that right.

***

The local news replays awkward clips from the interview all day long, and the phone won't stop ringing. I finally turn the ringer off, because I'm not planning to answer the phone anyway.

Papi hasn't been able to look for work because reporters have been following him, which prevents any customers from hiring him for odd jobs. Mami hasn't gone back to work either. Her boss fired her for "not having papers." As if he hadn't always known.

We have no income, but the lawyer said we're okay. She brought us a check for two thousand dollars, which she says came from some online donation account. My parents paid rent three weeks late, paid a few people who loaned them money, and said they still owe a lot more so all that was left was enough for standard bean tacos.

I can't do this anymore. I miss the flavor of Josue's cooking, and when I close my eyes at night, I see his face. I smell the pomegranate and orange trees when the wind blows, even though they're not really there. But I also love standing next to Mami and seeing the look of relief in Papi's eyes every morning when he checks to confirm that I'm still here. Brenden and Esteban are acting weird, but they've been on their own for a month while I was gone. They don't know what to say to me.

It's okay. I don't know what to say to them either. But I'm working on it.

A knock at the door jars me from my thoughts. I stand up and look through the peephole.

Ms. Lilia Marquez.

FORTY-THREE

In the end, our fancy lawyer couldn't protect us from the swift actions of the department of immigration. Ms. Lilia Marquez was good at getting me in front of the camera, and my face has been plastered all over the television and internet. People from across the country have weighed in. Everyone has an opinion.

Apparently, it's my fault for being deported. I shouldn't have been running near the border. I shouldn't have lied about my age or where I was from when they threatened to deport Mami. I should have escaped from Josue.

But the other half of the internet says it never should have happened.

I sigh. It did happen.

I think about all the things that I wish hadn't happened. But that's the thing. It's complicated. Because the one thing that I think should not have happened, above and beyond all the little and big things that have happened, is the one thing that keeps replaying in my mind. I close my eyes and see Josue falling to the ground. Again. The memory is on repeat, although the scenery and the sounds keep changing.

"Mami, where will we live?" I ask.

Mami is standing beside me folding clothes. I watch as she adds another pair of Brenden's jeans to the open suitcase in front of her. She doesn't look up from her task. "We were offered a visa move to Canada."

"Really?"

"The world has been watching, Shayla."

Wait a minute. We're not going to Guatemala? We'll all be legal somewhere?

"When are we leaving?"

"Tomorrow."

I think about all the things I never got to do. I never saw the ocean. I'm behind in school. I never had a boyfriend, although…

"Canada?"

I think back to what the officers told me. Stockholm Syndrome. No, I never had a boyfriend. Just a Coyote who apparently had a gun. An older man who liked me more than he should have.

But that doesn't mean I don't miss him, in some odd way. I don't know how long it will take to recover, but it feels like these wounds will heal much more slowly than my broken ankle.

"How will we pay for it?" I ask.

"Shayla, *mija*, stop worrying. The website raised money for us. We'll get an apartment and settle in. Everything will be okay." She looks up at me finally, and I instantly feel like I've been punched in the gut. Silent tears are trailing down her cheeks in a slow, winding river.

I'm not sure which one of us reached out first, but soon her arms are wrapped around me.

***

"Shayla!"

I turn to the growing crowd, and I know that they're expecting something from me. But I'm not really sure what I have to offer. Cameras flash and more people call my name.

My spine tenses and I slowly twist around to face the people who have come here to see us leave. To say goodbye.

This was my country.

It is still my brothers' country. It isn't really mine anymore. And it definitely isn't Mami's or Papi's country. And from what they told me last night, we have nowhere to return to.

There are hundreds of men and women standing behind the barricade. Maybe more than that. I see so many faces, and some are holding signs. "Save Shayla!" says one. "*Queremos justicia!*" declares another.

I used to want to get out of my small town more than anything. Every ounce of my existence was based on finding a way to get me and my family out of there. I would've found a way.

Mami and Papi turn and pause beside me. Should I speak? These are the people that fought for us. For me. "It's okay, Shayla," Papi says softly. "You don't owe them anything." Mami nods beside him.

I glance over at my little brothers. They both look so much taller now. Less squirrely. My absence changed them. I reach over and ruffle Brenden's hair.

"You're right," I tell Papi. "I don't owe them anything." I clear my throat. "I owe this to myself."

I step away from them, just mere feet from the airport entrance. We could've left quietly. But it turns out, I'm not the quiet girl who I used to be. I move closer to the crowd and take a deep breath. And another.

"Hi." My voice is unsteady, and I know that I won't be able to speak over the crowd. But then, one of them shushes the crowd and suddenly everyone falls silent. "I appreciate what you guys have done for me," I say. "And I wish we could stay. My parents deserve amnesty, but this country won't recognize the tragedies that they escaped from."

I peer out into the audience, looking from one face to the next. Teens like me, with hope in their eyes. The crowd is a mixture of people who mostly look like me, but there are others. There are people with lighter and darker skin. Old and young. I release my death grip on my roll-on suitcase and fold my arms over my chest.

"We want to stay. But that's not an option."

***

In the front row stands a girl who looks just like Cara, the girl I met at the border. I stare at her for a moment, and realize it isn't actually her. But her eyes, the way they bore into me. This girl that is not Cara is holding a #SaveShayla sign high above her head. I imagine all the girls like her, standing at the other edge of the border. Trying to figure out a safe way to cross. Or at least, a safe enough way.

"It was wrong for them to assume that I was undocumented just because I'm a Latina," I say, my voice rising. "It was wrong for them to threaten to deport my parents if I didn't claim another country." Somewhere in the crowd, someone cheers my name. A few fists rise in the air. "It was wrong for them to order for my parents to leave the country, just because they were embarrassed by all the media attention. It was wrong for them to force me to leave just because I was scared and signed a form."

Esteban appears at my side, and he wraps his tiny arm around my waist. "I'm an American by birth," I say. "But now, I have no country. This place has turned its back on me and my family."

A roar courses through the crowd.

"I played by the rules. I got good grades, I participated in athletics, and I had a job. I listened to my parents and did whatever they asked. I did everything right. And it wasn't enough to save my family." My eyes are heavy with tears, but I bite my lip. Those tears don't belong to this crowd. They are mine and only mine.

"We want to stay. But we are strong and brave, and we can survive anywhere."

"SHAYLA!" someone calls from the back of the crowd. Cheers continue. I pause, waiting for the sound of the crowd to die down. "*JUSTICIA!*" someone screams.

"But for your sakes, all of you," I tell them, "Keep fighting. Keep standing against this injustice. I'm probably not the first, and I won't be the last. Fight for people like my parents and my brothers. And me."

I smile and shout their word in Spanish as loud as I can. "*JUSTICIA!*" My fist rises in the air, and I feel both my brothers at my side, copying my movement. I've got a long way to go until I can speak my parents' language, but I'm ready to start learning. More importantly, they're ready to let me learn.

"Thank you!" I yell, and I hug both boys to my sides. I glance back at my parents, who are hovering in the doorway. "We have to go," I say to my brothers quietly.

The crowd screams and I see the tension on the faces of police officers at the front of the lines. I know that it's time to leave. It hurts; every single plan I'd ever had was set on following the rules.

"Ready?" I ask the boys. I shift the backpack over my shoulder. They nod, and we turn to walk towards the airport doorway. The crowd continues chanting behind us as we pass through the awaiting double doors.

Mami is standing at the ticket counter, weighing her luggage. "It'll be an adventure," I tell my brothers. Esteban grins, and Brenden looks at me strangely.

"Like when that bad man kept you?"

I shake my head sadly. "No, Bren." The lady at the counter hands my mom a stack of tickets. Papi starts to walk towards us. "Better. We can even eat bean tacos for breakfast."

He scrunches up his nose. "But I don't like bean tacos," he whispers loudly.

I wrap my arms around my Papi, grateful that I've found my way home. Because as it turns out, wherever my family is will be enough for me. Wherever we're going will be enough. "Let's go," I say, and we start walking towards airport security. Whatever lies ahead of us will be enough.

My lawyer was right. I need to heal. We all need to heal.

One thing remains certain, one truth. I glance over at my little brothers and smile sadly. I don't think I'll ever be able to see the world the same again, because it will never be the same. I will always be the girl who got deported. The girl who needed a Coyote to come home. The girl who fell for a dangerous man.

I sigh. I know this one thing is true.

Nunca te olvidaré, Josue.

PREVIEW

The Caravan Series:
Book 1: Corriendo (Running)
January 2020

"Itzel," I said cheerfully. "I got in!"

"That's wonderful," my best friend shouted in my ear. We were standing together on the corner near the town square, and a band played loudly in the distance. It was a festival day, Tres Reyes, and everyone was wearing their absolute best outfits. I'd just gotten off work and we were walking up the cobblestone road towards my house. I couldn't wait to get home to open presents and enjoy warm fruit punch with tamales that my Mami and I had prepared over the past several days. Each one was wrapped in a large banana leaf and tied with a piece of thick yarn. Opening them was always more magical than opening gifts.

The sound of fireworks came from just ahead of us. That was odd; no one in my neighborhood usually used firecrackers on festival days. They were cheery, but expensive. I smiled at Itzel. "Maybe my brother is starting the party early?"

We began racing up the hill; both of in our matching brown dresses from the touristic coffee shop that we worked at on weekends. I'd pulled an extra shift for the holiday, and Itzel had already been on schedule. We must've looked so carefree in that moment; our matching braids flopping back and forth as we ran, the woven fabric of our village weaved carefully into each of our side braids. Our smiles were probably those giddy, schoolgirl contagious smiles that can break a band of us into abrupt laughter and joy of all things that come with the crossing over from childhood into young womanhood.

Another loud popping sound came from up ahead. I laughed. They hadn't waited for us at all. Itzel reached my doorway first, and when she turned the handle, the door sucked inward. Like it had a life of its own. She entered two feet ahead of me, her happy dimples shining on each cheek.

I want to always remember her that way; not the way that she looked mere seconds after. As I followed her inside, we both recognized too late that we hadn't been hearing firecrackers. A masked man saw both of us and aimed his gun in our direction. "Johama, no!" Itzel called out, abruptly pushing me into the wall as a stream of bullets bombarded her perfect body. She fell immediately; her dark red blood gushing into little rivers around her torso.

I clung to the wall, not ready for my fate. "Please don't hurt me," I begged.

I didn't know yet that there were far worse ways to be hurt than the sudden way that Itzel was taken from me.

ABOUT THE AUTHOR

Sheryl Recinos is a family physician practicing as a hospitalist in Los Angeles, California. She volunteers with migrant patients and has been active as an advocate for human rights and migrant healthcare.

She is the author of the Resilience Group middle school series and is releasing a YA series focusing on the plight of migrant youth as they try to find their way to safety.

Her debut book was her memoir about surviving teen homelessness, which has won several awards; *Hindsight: Coming of age on the streets of Hollywood.*

Made in the USA
Lexington, KY
10 December 2019

58375062R00146